Imagine a Shared Economy...

In which all people have access to food, clothing, affordable housing, living-wage jobs, medical care, education, and opportunities to improve their lives, while living sustainably on a planet on which:

- The condition of the environment is improving

- Local economies are vibrant, democracy is growing stronger, a greater sense of community is developing in cities and towns, small businesses are flourishing, family farmers are profitable, poverty is in sharp decline, and children do not go to bed hungry

- The economically powerful special interests that receive favorable treatment from governments are communities, rather than lobbyists for wealthy private interests

- The purpose of the shared economic system is not to produce maximum profits and growth for the few, but adequate profits and sustainable growth for the good of all—to create a brighter future

Is this a utopian dream? You may not think so when you read this book.

If you are open to the idea that a new beginning is possible, this just might be what you've been looking for!

D1533902

*Imagine a society with commun
corporations, and people more valued than profits. Many
have imagined it. Now we can create it.*

From E2M.org Social Brochure – Sept. 2007

Acknowledgements

This book has been in the making for a lifetime. The concepts forwarded within its pages come following a lifetime of education in agriculture, the sciences, invention, entrepreneurship, manufacturing, community development, and observations of the human condition.

I would like to thank my wonderful wife Irene who has never wavered in her faith, delivered peacefulness into my life, and gave me my daughters Robin and Annie. It is with them that I learned about the joy of family and how to become a loving husband and father. I thank my mother Marjorie Guzelian for being there in the early years when she was my anchor in a turbulent and challenging sea that could have consumed both of us had it not been for her strength.

During my business career, I learned many of the concepts that allowed me to understand what was necessary to write this book. Many thanks to my mentors, hundreds of loyal employees, and those who invested in any way in that education.

The most important part of my life came when I ended my years as a commercial entrepreneur and became a social entrepreneur. Thanks to Joanne Campbell, at the Valley Community Development Corporation for giving me the platform there to hone my community development skills and to learn what possibilities existed.

Thanks to those economists, elected officials, entrepreneurs, labor leaders, pastors, students, and others named within these pages who were the earliest supporters of the ideas within these pages.

Eternal prayers and appreciation to the late Julie Anne Graham. She was my friend, teacher, student, collaborator, patron, board member, and inspiration to write this book.

Very special thanks go to Mary Westervelt, David Bisson, and Ed Bisson, for investing years of their time, enthusiasm, faith, and money to move these ideas from the written word to the reality of a working group, non-profit organization, and economic template that we feel could help bring about positive change on a wide scale basis.

Thanks also to Roz Malkin who came more recently to help me see that our ultimate success could only come if we extended our vision from within our backyard to beyond the horizon.

Last, but certainly not least, I am thankful for the Universal Energy many of us know as God, Allah, Great Spirit, Creator, or Almighty who lays the path for all of us and who makes it visible to the faithful who ask to see it and commit to walk it.

To Charles + Hong,

Thank you for being part
of our lives and businesses...
And we thought it was all
about neon. Ha Ha.

This is what it is <u>really</u>
about.

Much Love,
Michel
11/23/2017.

COMMUNITY CAPITALISM

How Communities Can Use Capitalism
to Create a Shared Economy
that Works for Everyone

TM

www.communitycapitalism.com
www.e2m.org

by Michael Garjian

Ten percent of author's profits go to help E2M.org create a shared economy

E2M.org • PO Box 188 • Easthampton, MA 01027 • info@e2m.org

Front Cover Art: Arthimedes, Illustrator/Vector Artist
Back Cover Art: Boguslaw Mazur, Illustrator / Vector Artist/Videographer

Table of Contents

Introduction

As is true of many people today, I feel things are not on a good path, socioeconomically or environmentally. However, I belong to that group of optimists who believe it is possible to create a world vastly different from the one we are currently experiencing. My own feeling is that we are at a fork in the path of the human journey. Our decision of which direction to travel will determine the future of the planet and the humans who occupy it.

I am writing this book after more than a decade of work as a social entrepreneur following four decades of work as a commercial entrepreneur manufacturing technologies that I invented. I believe the information I am offering here can provide solutions to a number of the most pressing problems we are experiencing in today's world.

In offering this information to you, it is important for me to note that I am not a scholar with a string of academic degrees attached to my name. The concepts in this book were not created by me after long, arduous, and thoughtful analysis of economic history, data, or current events. In fact, I might be considered by academics to be an unlikely source of such information. I received this information as an epiphany following the closure of my last factory on August 30, 1999. However, this information did not come as a sudden flash of inspiration; it came to me in various forms over a period of several months in bits and pieces of information, hints and hunches, philosophical fragments, and flashes of inspiration.

For these reasons, I initially felt some reluctance to present such ideas; however, a significant number of people with impeccable credentials have asked me to ignore my reservations and press onward. They advised me to write from the heart, using my life experiences as my educational platform. These experiences, they assured me, serve me more adequately for this endeavor than might a nonentrepreneurial scholarly platform expounding on theories without any practical experience. Thus, I deliver this information not as an academic but as a common man writing for common people.

I have been assured by other creative writers, musicians, and artists that although many wonderful poems, songs, and symphonies come from diligent, thoughtful, and time-consuming efforts, in other instances these works come as a tune that suddenly starts playing in a musician's mind, or the vision that comes in a painter's dreams, or the storyline that comes from an unexpected flash of inspiration. They tell me these works come from a special place, not to be questioned, but simply to be humbly accepted and unselfishly delivered.

That is the purpose of this book. I consider it to be a gift of information given to me to be passed on to you. If this information leads to something interesting, helpful, or even wonderful, it will be because you and others found something compelling within its pages that you felt was worth acting on, as an individual, as a community.

If that does happen, then we may even accomplish what I have come to believe – that together we can create the society that many of us have been hoping and praying for. As an optimist, the ideas I am presenting in this book may appear to be utopian in nature, so a brief personal introduction is in order.

As a commercial entrepreneur turned social entrepreneur, during my sixty-nine years, I have owned a number of manufacturing businesses producing inventions I developed.

Since August 30, 1999, when I closed my last factory and become a social entrepreneur, I have been recognized publicly for my work helping many low-income entrepreneurs start businesses; teaching tenant associations of large, low income housing complexes how to use their financial power to achieve their social agendas; my work in indoor farming; and my part in developing technologies capable of converting many forms of biomass into bio-carbon and biofuels while removing carbon from the atmosphere.

I spent my childhood as a laborer on an egg farm that housed 40,000 chickens. My dreams of becoming an inventor came true when I was accepted at the University of Massachusetts in Amherst, Mass. where I studied business, physics, and science. In the thirty years following my college graduation in 1969, I employed more than 400 associates in the U.S. and abroad manufacturing my technologies which earned me nine domestic and international patents and a joint venture with what was the largest company in the world in 1992.

During the late 1970s my interest was in plasma physics. This resulted in my invention, in 1985, of flat, light-emitting plates of glass just over a quarter-inch thick containing a plasma similar to that in today's compact fluorescent lamps that are now replacing incandescent bulbs.

By engraving artistic images into a plate of glass, then fusing another glass plate onto the engraved plate, I was able to create sealed cavities inside the fused plates. I then filled the cavities with the light emitting plasma, resulting in my creation of the world's first flat glass, tubeless, neon signs. That invention was acclaimed by leading industry journals as the most significant advance in neon sign fabrication since their invention by Georges Claude in Paris in 1912.

In addition to the flat light source, I co-patented the world's first viable solid-state power supply for neon signs and plasma light sources. My company, Neon Technology Corporation, sold these signs to numerous Fortune 500 companies around the world. That led to my formation, in 1996, of a joint venture with the largest company in the world, at their request.

However, in 1998, global investors saw they could make a higher rate of return elsewhere, so they withdrew billions of investment dollars from Asia, resulting in the collapse of the Asian economy–and subsequently the joint venture. This severely impacted Neon Technology. I was unable to access any equity investors because they were enamored with dotcom companies. They felt that manufacturing companies could not produce the returns that dotcoms could.

Of course, we now see that they were wrong. The result was the collapse of the Internet technology sector and the loss of many manufacturing companies, including Neon Technology. I reluctantly closed my U.S. manufacturing facility on August 30, 1999, after securing employment for all my employees in a friend's company.

After decades of high-stress manufacturing, I vividly recall walking down the hall and leaving the Neon Technology factory for the last time. I very emphatically said "OK God, I'm not interested in inventing any more objects – no more factories, no weight, no freight, no more employees. I'd like an idea, something that can fly around the world effortlessly and do good." Upon that exhortation, I continued walking and never looked back.

During the next month, I took a little time away from work-related matters to catch my breath. I wanted to re-evaluate the world around me with more clarity than is afforded to one constrained by the walls of a factory employing scores of people producing a tangible product. That resulted in my observation that, on a socioeconomic level, things were not going in a good direction for the vast majority of the populace. Thus, I made the decision to change my direction from commercial entrepreneurship to social entrepreneurship.

During that period, I responded to an ad in the classifieds looking for someone to re-establish the small business and economic development department of the Valley Community Development Corporation, a non-profit organization in Western Massachusetts. I knew I could deliver a positive result for the organization. After being hired, from 2000 to 2005, I helped my low income clients start seventy businesses in the local community. I also arranged close to half a million dollars in loans for my entrepreneurial clients. Every one of them had been declined for loans from traditional financial institutions, so I arranged loans from secondary lending organizations. My work at the Valley CDC earned me several awards. It is well-documented in numerous newspaper and business journal articles, one of which credited my office as one of the three most significant catalysts for the economic renaissance of Easthampton, Mass.

During the period from August 1999 and December 1999, in addition to taking the position at the Valley CDC, I was finally able to articulate a vision resulting from my receipt of the aforementioned bits of information. To my astonishment, it was a vision of an alternative economic model quite different from the models of capitalism, socialism, or communism with which I was most familiar. The model was certainly not socialism or communism because it had a free-market foundation. It was also not traditional capitalism because it did not embrace of the current model of capitalism that is bent on achieving maximum profits and maximum growth for relatively few investors regardless of the impact on the community or the planet.

The model I was envisioning was based on achieving adequate profits and sustainable growth for the good of everyone. Its goal was not based on the greed of the current system, but on a model of sharing investment returns and caring for each other – a shared economy, if you will. In any event, I saw this vision as a gift, an answer to my request for an idea. As a gift, I felt it was my obligation to pass it on to you. That is the purpose of this book.

I formalized my commitment to social entrepreneurship on January 1, 2000 in my home studio in Easthampton, Mass. where I wrote the first words of a personal manifesto to change my direction in life and dedicate myself to a new mission to advance this new economic model. I decided that perhaps it was best not to include the model I was envisioning among any of the existing "isms." So, considering that it was January 1, 2000, I gave it the three letter internet designation E2M, which stood for Economic Model for Millennium 2000. I secured the domain name E2M.org that morning and set my pen to paper at 11:00 a.m. to write my first thoughts about the path upon which I had been placed. Those first writings are available at www.e2m.org.

During the next three months, I discussed these ideas with a number of friends, educators, economists, elected officials, UMass administrators, labor leaders, community members, and students. I found overwhelming support and was encouraged to form an organization to move these ideas forward. Thus I formed e2m.org as a nonprofit organization.

In a nutshell, the E2M model can be defined as a shared economy composed of a network of decentralized, regional economic communities, each controlled by a local nonprofit Regional Economic Council (REC) composed of community members who are demographically representative of the local region. The purpose of each REC is to be a repository of community wealth, which will be used to serve the best interests of the regional community. These RECs are independent of each other but are linked by the national E2M.org which acts as the chartering and facilitating organization. This national organization gives birth to each REC and enables the disparate regions to assist each other and act collectively where desirable. E2M.org also administers the E2M administrative website as well as the future E2M networking website, which is the portal for the general populace to enter the E2M inspired shared economic system. This shared economy will include community members, businesses, credit unions, investors, charitable organizations, product lines, and other entities.

Because it came as more of a revelation than a research project, when I first wrote about E2M, I did not draw on the work of others. Virtually all of this freely flowing material was original work in 2000. The material in this book comes from three sources– my original writings from 2000 to 2004; a lecture I was invited to give at the Boston Social Forum in July 2004; and a talk I delivered at the Relocalization Conference in Western Massachusetts in September 2007.

Some of these ideas are now being written about by others because events I predicted back then are now beginning to come about. Thus, as I now write this book, I will not footnote any more recent work that postdates mine. Considering this lack of footnotes, I chose another method to support these ideas: I am including quotations from diverse individuals over centuries to support my contentions and to provide what my editors say is enjoyable and highly appropriate content.

I hope you will find as much inspiration in these pages as I have in taking this journey. I humbly present this book for your consideration as a manifesto and road map to the next era that must come if we, as a loving and caring human race, are to succeed on our collective journey to our true destiny.

That destiny is not within the current system of corporate capitalism whose purpose is to maximize profits and growth for the few at the expense of the environment, planet, and the billions of souls who populate it. That system, with its excessive focus on profits, growth, consumerism, and ever-increasing observation and control of the populace by the few, cannot be our destiny because it is both inequitable and financially unsustainable.

Our destiny is also not dependent on making "some" changes to the current system to make it more acceptable. We cannot tweak the system around the edges with the hopes it will become something we all hope for. It is so dysfunctional, disordered, and corrupted that it is neither capable, nor even worthy, of true, honest, long-term positive change. For these reasons, it is evident that our true destiny lies in another paradigm with another system, a system dedicated primarily to the well-being of people and communities, not just to that of shareholders and corporations.

To reach our true human destiny requires that we create a new economic paradigm, a shared economy, which can provide a long-term, sustainable, and dignified future for our entire planet and all its inhabitants. In such a shared economy it is possible for all people to have food, water, clothing, shelter, medical care, an education, and opportunities for personal advancement and community.

The shared economy is not an unattainable future era we might achieve some time in the indeterminate future when we, as humans, have evolved to a higher life form, or when we have developed extraordinary new technologies that will free us from the limitations that now restrict us.

A shared economy is neither a utopian vision realizable only when governments, powerful elites, or other outside entities create it for us; nor is it a creation possible only in the minds of dreamers. A shared economy does not require the permission of any of those entities, nor is it a dream. It is within our reach. We can have it anytime we want it. We can have it now. The shared economy is ours for the taking.

Some of us are already assembling the pieces, and this book is your invitation to join those of us who are already building the new foundations. This book is not more of the same tiresome rhetoric asking you not to give up hope, or pleading for you to dream of greater things. *This book is a detailed roadmap to the shared economy.* And the best news is that the path to the shared economy is not a complex myriad of streets, avenues, U-turns, and forks in the road. It is a straight line, simple to follow path we can execute – in years, not decades or centuries!

This book is dedicated to the young –to those who are the most important group in achieving the shared economy. You are the most important generation in the history of humanity. You are the ones who will decide if this planet will ultimately be controlled by large multinational corporations whose primary mission is to maximize profits and growth for relatively few, regardless of environmental and human impacts, or if it will be controlled by communities to serve the common good and achieve a sustainable society and dignified life for everyone.

The outcomes on humanity of these two possibilities are very different: The decision may even be the calling of your generation. I truly hope that something within these pages will inspire my reader to act to achieve the better of those two possibilities.

Michael Garjian

The wisdom of the wise and the experience of the ages are perpetuated by quotations.

~ Benjamin Disraeli

Not only is another world possible, she is on her way. On a quiet day, I can hear her breathing.

~ Arundhati Roy, Indian novelist;
winner of Sydney Peace Prize

When real music comes to me - the music of the spheres, the music that surpasses understanding - that music has nothing to do with me, cause I'm just the channel. The only joy for me is for it to be given to me, and to transcribe it like a medium...those moments are what I live for.

~ John Lennon

Put the argument into a concrete shape, into an image, some hard phrase, round and solid as a ball, which they can see and handle and carry home with them, and the cause is half won.

~ Ralph Waldo Emerson

The most important thing to remember is this: To be ready at any moment to give up what you are for what you might become.

~ W. E. B. Du Bois

In life, many thoughts are born in the course of a moment, an hour, a day. Some are dreams, some visions. Often, we are unable to distinguish between them. To some, they are the same; however, not all dreams are visions. Much energy is lost in fanciful dreams that never bear fruit. But visions are messages from the Great Spirit, each for a different purpose in life. Consequently, one person's vision may not be that of another. To have a vision, one must be prepared to receive it, and when it comes, to accept it. Thus when these inner urges become reality, only then can visions be fulfilled. The spiritual side of life knows everyone's heart and who to trust. How could a vision ever be given to someone to harbor if that person could not be trusted to carry it out. The message is simple: commitment precedes vision.

~ High Eagle, Native American musician and
Presidential Medal of Freedom Recipient

Chapter 1 – A Fork in the Path

To begin, it's important to know that this is not about me. It's never been about me; it cannot be about me; it must be about us. I am simply a messenger. This is about freedom. For some, it can be freedom from hunger, poverty, homelessness, and hopelessness. For others, it is freedom from environmental decline or social malaise. For many more of us, it is freedom from a lifestyle of ever-increasing speed yet diminishing happiness. For all of us, it could be freedom from the damage being done to us and our planet by an economic system driven by human greed. I believe it is the freedom to choose a future that works for all of us rather than for just a few. It is the freedom of individual and community self-determination.

This book is about a very powerful tool that will enable communities to become more powerful than large corporations, and people to become more valued than profits. Some people who walked this path with me even feel it will enable us enter a new chapter in the human narrative. They feel we might be on the path to a new era that could come about as we all create a shared economy. Such an era might even be called the Community Age in which the dominant economic forces on this planet are families and communities, not billionaires and large multinational corporations.

I believe that hunger, poverty, homelessness, and many forms of ill-health are unnatural, created by the current economic system of corporate capitalism that was created by the few to serve themselves at the expense of the many. It is an economic system unfortunately based on human greed. I am one of those people who believe it is possible to create a society in which everyone has a dignified lifestyle with access to food, shelter, clothing, medical care, education, and opportunities to improve themselves. I am also of the belief that this can only be achieved if we reevaluate the way we currently do things and understand that change is possible.

I do not mean change brought about by overseers such as governments, politicians, corporations, or other agencies. I mean real change that we can bring about ourselves, just by deciding to do it. It is change we can bring about without spending much of our time or money, especially since most of us don't have much time or money anymore. It is also change that can achieve the society of a shared economy that works for everyone.

We all know the current situation is not acceptable for the vast majority of us. Many people now see the folly of living lives of excessive consumption and debt, which go hand in hand. Yet for them this realization comes too late; the treadmill of life continues to accelerate in speed. Due to recent events in the world economic community, it is becoming increasingly obvious that the masses are subservient to a ruling class of financial elites.

These elites live lives of uber-extravagance funded by the masses through taxes, manipulation of the currency, mortgage interest payments, usury, excessive credit card interest rates, and billions of dollars received from insidious bank fees, bailouts and bonus plans. Those of us who provide them their lifestyles work harder and harder each year while going deeper and deeper in debt, if not poverty. For many, expenses continue to exceed income regardless of any increases in wages. Millions of us are losing our homes, pensions, and retirement savings. Many more are just staying afloat. Some of us have even worked all our lives, then lost it all when the economy tanked and the value of assets plummeted. With the added news of climate change and its effects, things can get pretty dreary for many people. And that's for the lucky few of us in industrialized countries. Others still spend all day just to find a cup of rice or a quart of clean water.

It is obviously time for a change.

At this point of human history, it is obvious to many of us that we are on the wrong path. Yet we are not at the end of a path, we are at a fork in the road. We can continue on our current path with predictable, yet undesirable, results or we can move in a new direction, taking the best of the past while embracing new ideas to create a shared economy and a sustainable and bright future for us all.

Technology and economics were the factors that led to the emergence of other great transitions such as the Agrarian, Industrial, and Information Ages. With the emergence of today's technologies of the Internet, cell phones, and tablets, there can be little doubt of what can be achieved. As one futurist said, the introduction of the Internet to humanity is as important as the introduction of language. Now, with the addition of cell phones and instant communication to millions for little expense, even more is possible on an unprecedented scale.

From an economic point of view, a shared economy based on achieving adequate profits and sustainable growth for the common good has far more to offer than a greed-based economic system that seeks maximum profit and growth for relatively few extremely wealthy investors, less than 1% of the entire population. As a community-conscious free-market economic model, the shared economy could help lead us into a new economic reality that works for everyone.

Those people who are happy with their current situations can continue to walk the current path. Many more of us now need to take the fork in the road heading to a fair, equitable, and sustainable economy. The world that billions of people have been praying for over the millennia is now possible; and we can all walk into a brighter future together. It awaits us whenever we want it and when together we make it happen.

It is now possible to create a shared economy in which communities are more powerful than corporations and people are more valued than profits; a shared economy devoid of poverty, hunger, homelessness, and hopelessness.

It is ours for the taking.

How wonderful it is that nobody need wait a single moment before starting to improve the world.

~Anne Frank

A moment comes, which comes but rarely in history, when we step out from the old to the new, when an age ends, and when the sound of a nation, long suppressed, finds utterance.

~Jawaharial Nehru, India's First Prime Minister

Believe nothing just because a so-called wise person said it. Believe nothing just because a belief is generally held. Believe nothing just because it is said in ancient books. Believe nothing just because it is said to be of divine origin. Believe nothing just because someone else believes it. Believe only what you yourself test and judge to be true.

~Buddha

Imagination is more important than knowledge. For while knowledge defines all we currently know and understand, imagination points to all we might yet discover and create.

~Albert Einstein

You may say I'm a dreamer, but I'm not the only one, I hope someday you will join us, and the world will live as one.

~John Lennon

Chapter 2 – Where Are We Now?

Recent events indicate a deep dissatisfaction by many people, particularly the young, in the condition of our society and planet. The Earth is threatened by climate disruptions. Over the past ten years, energy costs have risen and global oil consumption may soon exceed global oil production. This has resulted in ever-increasing costs of food, energy, and anything produced using energy. Real unemployment in many countries is at alarming levels. Students are saddled with lifelong student loan debts they cannot repay because of the lack of jobs. Dissatisfaction with socioeconomic and political realities is resulting in civil unrest. A massive new movement called the Arab Spring has toppled long established dictatorships in Arab nations. In the USA, the younger generation expressed its anger when the Occupy Wall Street initiative captured the imagination of millions of people young and old around the globe. It is obvious that millions of people are tired of being victims of multinational corporate greed, a corrupted banking system, a dysfunctional political system, and massive inequities of wealth. Economists are even warning that this era may be the beginning of the collapse of the modern day banking and economic system.

Stories about social, economic, and environmental degradation seem to dominate today's news – climate change, increasing poverty and hunger, homelessness, economic chaos, and record unemployment. We have seen trillions of dollars spent on bailouts and bonuses for banks and rich investors, all funded by taxes collected from a middle class in ruin. We are angered even more as our taxes are being used to pay huge salaries and bonuses to bankers as they foreclose on millions of our homes, oftentimes because of those same bankers' greed, mistakes and even corrupt manipulation of the economic system they created. These are also the same bankers who chose not to lift a finger to help millions of homeowners whom they duped into taking mortgages they could not afford. As the truth comes out, it seems that the hopes of the many are being smothered by the greed of the few. We worry for the innocent young, our children, who must eventually pay for it all as taxes collected by a government growing in size and power. Many of us feel that the possibility of a brighter future for our children and ourselves grows dimmer while society moves down a path headed in the wrong direction.

Recently, revolutions have erupted in Egypt, Libya, Tunisia, and Syria. These upheavals, once called the Arab Spring, have resulted in the demise of long-held dictatorships. Other such dictatorships remain very fragile, and greater changes are coming. Major protests against world financial organizations such as the World Bank and the International Monetary Fund have erupted in Greece as it teeters on the brink of bankruptcy. Italy is not far behind. Any number of circumstances could lead to the fall of other leaders, governments, national economies, and even the European Union. If these events come to pass, the United States and the global economy will not be spared the harsh effects.

Many would say these are times that demand a reevaluation of where we are headed as a society and whether we are on a path to a future that works for everyone or for just the few. If we continue on the current path, the rich will get richer and more powerful, multinational corporations bent on maximizing profits for the few will become even more powerful, and the political sector will become more coopted, coming under greater control of increasingly powerful economic forces.

As new technologies are developed, we will see significant advances in medicines and medical procedures, longer lifespans, and other positive advances to help people; however that will be accompanied by more effective observation and control of the populace, more precise techniques to deliver deadly force in general warfare or against individuals, and increasing amounts of work done by robots or other not yet developed technologies. We are already seeing job losses due to replacement of humans by robots; and as robotic technology improves during the next decade or two, even more jobs will be lost.

Considering the fact that people earn money by doing work, we must ask how the masses will support themselves when there is much less work to do. Will they become wards of the state? What form would a government take if it were responsible for supporting millions of people? Who would control that government? These are valid questions we must think about, for we are on the path to that reality now.

Legally endowed with the constitutional rights of individuals, corporations were able to amass great control within the economic and democratic infrastructure of America and other countries. Having the sole mission of producing maximum profits and growth for their investors, massive corporations are engaging in behaviors that many believe to be contrary to the interests of the community and planet. As corporations and their investors develop more economic power and control over the planet, individuals, communities, and smaller countries take a back seat. Democracy, as an institution, has become so negatively impacted by special interests that vast numbers of people in the general population have stopped voting in the U.S.

As technologies have been developed and implemented, the efficiencies they introduce have resulted in the increase of individual productivity, longer working hours, and the reduction of jobs. Technological advances have failed to reduce workplace stress and increase the leisure time of the populace as was once imagined. At the very early stages of computer development, it was said a computer would be able to do as much work in an hour as a person could in a week; thus a new age of leisure was coming for the benefit of humanity. However, as we have seen, the reality became that one person using a computer could do much more work in a week for the same pay, produce even more profits, and reduce the number of employees necessary. Not surprisingly, the "age of leisure" became a victim of the capitalist need to maximize profits and growth for the few. This will be true of all future technologies unless there is a systemic change in the economic system.

As technologies develop further, the ability of investors and corporations to reign in those who might oppose them grows. The advances in life sciences, robotics and nanotechnology leave significant room for misuse of emerging technologies such as artificial intelligence, brain wave sensors, microscopic cameras, genetic engineering of plant or other forms of life, and the Internet, to name an important few.

On January 21, 2010 the U.S. Supreme Court voted, under the Citizens United decision, to lift all bans on the amount of money corporations may spend on the campaigns of political candidates. This reverses one hundred years of protections against such corporate influence in elections and ushers in a new era for the advancement of corporate control over the social and governmental sector in America. This new ruling also applies to U.S. corporations owned by foreign nationals, enemies of our country, or others who may not have the best interests of America in mind. We are truly standing on a slippery slope.

My feeling is that during the first three decades of this millennium, it will be determined who will control the planet Earth – corporations and billionaires with a lust for profits, or communities and families with a lust for life. I think current experience indicates the control must go to communities and families. Despite many inequities brought about since 1850 the beginning of the Industrial Age and subsequent Information and Technology Age, those eras have helped lay the foundation for a great new age, the Community Age. This could be a sustainable era in which economic power and democracy are in the control of communities and used to advance the common good. Technologies would be used to lighten the human load and increase times of leisure rather than increasing the productivity of the working class to benefit the wealthy.

I believe one path in the fork in the human journey leads to a future dominated by the billionaire class and multinational corporations with the indebted masses reliant on the government or other entities for their essential needs. The other path, I believe, can definitely take us to a future in which communities are as wealthy and powerful as corporations. A future in which communities are the powerful economic forces that control governments. A future in which communities, in partnership with entrepreneurs, own community-conscious companies that are dedicated to serving the community and its people, just as today's multinationals exist to serve their investors. A future in which such community-conscious companies are perpetually healthy because they have the overwhelming support of millions of people who want their products and embrace their missions. And, most important, A future in which these community-conscious companies introduce new technologies in nanoscience, robotics, and other technologies, not to subjugate the populace, but to provide services, benefits, financial dividends, and a more leisurely life to the community members whose support ensures their continued commercial success.

Although there is ample reason to be pessimistic about the future, I believe the current malaise is being visited upon us, at this critical moment in the evolution of humanity, to make the choice we face very clear. We can continue on this path, which is unsustainable and dangerous to humans and the planet, or we can move into an age in which the rise of community capitalism leads to the establishment of a shared economy that works for everyone in a bright and hopeful future for all.

I choose the latter. The purpose of this book is to lay out an easy to understand and execute initiative that we can use to get us there, not sometime in the indeterminate future, but starting right now. It requires no permission from any government, no approval from those who control the current economy, no legislation. It requires only our desire to get there. It is ours for the taking.

My intention is to first look at why this current system is unsustainable and is destined to fail, then to detail how a sustainable new shared economy based on the E2M economic model can end and eventually reverse the damage caused by the current system. You will also see how we have already created a template for a pilot E2M-based regional shared economy here in Western Massachusetts, complete with all the policies, procedures, by-laws, articles of organization and other materials necessary for you to easily form such a community in your region.

You will see how we can link E2M regional shared economies together to form a global shared economic network to serve the common good. Finally, you will see how a broader E2M-based shared economic system could relate to existing demographic sectors and institutions such as women, youth, faith-based organizations, unions, farmers, governments, municipalities, universities and colleges, and other relevant segments of our society, as well as emerging nations grass roots social movements, and very importantly, the world's major religions.

This is our shared economy; we can create it without the need for legislation or the permission of any government, legislative body, agency or person.

There is no time to waste; our time is now. So let's move ahead and see just how we as individuals, families, and communities can take our future into our own hands and on our own terms. It is ours for the taking!

It takes a lot of courage to release the familiar and seemingly secure, to embrace the new. But there is no real security in what is no longer meaningful. There is more security in the adventurous and exciting, for in movement there is life, and in change there is power.

~Alan Cohen, Author of 'Chicken Soup for the Soul'

It's a healthy thing now and then to hang a question mark on the things you have long taken for granted.
~Bertrand Russell

We can have a democratic society or we can have great wealth concentrated in the hands of a few. We cannot have both.
~Supreme Court Justice Louis Brandeis

Chapter 3 - Another World is Possible

Text of author's speech on September, 2007
Relocalization Conference – Northampton, Mass.

When I was a young boy growing up on the farm, sometimes when I was taking a short rest during my chores the boss would shout "Don't just stand there, do something!" His insensitivity grated on me in those days, but it's practical advice for us right now. Over the past 30 years, economically and politically, we have been experiencing some profound changes that are going in a very bad direction. We have no more time to just talk about these things, we need to actually get out there and do something, and we need to do it starting right now.

Many of the problems we are hearing about are the result of one root cause that is economic in nature. The root cause is that, within our current economic system, the criteria for investment is to seek maximum profit and maximum growth for the investor. Investors demand maximized economic growth of the Gross Domestic Product (GDP) as well as corporate profits and growth.

Now, profitability and growth are not enough. It's about *maximum* profits and growth. If investors achieve maximum profits and growth this year, they want to achieve even more profits and growth next year, ad infinitum. The issue that is really critical here is that corporations are required by law to achieve maximum profits and growth for the investors, otherwise those investors can sue them. How do these corporate criteria for investment root their way throughout our entire society? How do corporations achieve maximum profits and growth?

Well, the first thing corporations can do is produce products and keep the prices as high as possible and costs as low as possible. Lower costs often mean lower quality raw materials, lower wages, no benefits, outsourcing, and layoffs when profits are down.

Another way that corporations can be profitable is by purchasing another corporation that is successful, that has sales, that has a long time workforce. They can buy that corporation, pillage it for its assets, lay off the workers, then keep only what they need – the sales and good assets. In fact, that is one of the quickest and most effective ways to book profits and growth, other than, of course, outright Enron-style lying.

Another thing they can do to maximize profits and growth is to create more products. If they create more products, they have to sell more products. What if there is no need for more products? They'll create more needs. And how do they create needs? That requires more commercials and more advertising, and sticking kids in front of televisions when they are two years old. You and I sit in front of that tube and 25% of the time we are watching it they are trying to sell us something.

When we create more needs and create more products, sales are up and that requires more resources. And if we use them up here or we use them up there, we'll just get more over there and there, but unfortunately the planet is round, and there is only one.

All this requires more energy; it produces more waste, more pollution, and results in less resources remaining. Less resources remaining results in resource depletion. Resource depletion could mean resource wars. Let's hope we don't get ourselves into one of those! And as this whole process goes on, the large and lean and mean get larger, leaner and even meaner.

The rich get richer and the middle class erodes and joins the poor. Wealth concentrates. Here's some interesting statistics:

- In 2001 in the USA, 1% of the population owned almost 50% of all the private property. Less than 9% owned almost 92% of all the private property.

- As of 2001, 1% owned 50% of all of the investible liquid capital.

- Of every 10,000 people in that year, 20 made more in the sales of stocks and bonds than the other 9,980 combined.

Most of the property and money in America is in the hands of relatively few people.

Now, for anybody who plays Monopoly, you know how much fun it is when everybody else has all the assets and cash, while you've got just Baltic Avenue and fifty bucks, hoping to make it to "Go" to pick up your two hundred dollar paycheck. And that's if you don't go to jail first! It's tough enough doing that in a game, never mind that it is happening in real life. Every child born without silver spoon in its mouth is playing that game from the day they are born!

As wealth concentrates, special interests infect the political process. When special interests infect the political process, ordinary people become cynical and stop voting. When ordinary people stop voting, the unelected take office. When the unelected take office, we lose our democracy.

That is the result of maximum profits and growth for few investors. This is the goal and foundation of our current economic system. It lives for this purpose –to create maximum profits and growth for the few.

Now you younger folks out there do not have to accept it. You can look at this and say "No Thanks!" Because we can do better. We are in the most important 25 years in the history of humanity. Starting in 1995, this is the most important 25 years because this period will decide who controls the planet – corporations or communities.

Younger folks will be the most powerful force in making that determination. In fact I believe it is the great calling of their generation. But we all need to act together and we need to act now. Our current economic system not only favors the corporations, it virtually guarantees them control.

On top of all of this, our economic system is unsustainable. It is already unraveling. Corporate capitalism is killing itself as well as the planet, and it does not know how to stop.

Anything that Ben Bernanke and elected officials do is simply rearranging the deck chairs on the *Titanic*. The rest of us can stand on that deck singing with the band, or we can sing a different tune and build the lifeboats.

We need to understand that this system not immutable. It is a construct of humans, and as such is subject to revision. It is easier to embark on new path than to waste time trying to repair the unrepairable and unworthy.

It is time to move in a new direction and build an alternative economic system that works compatibly within the current system of corporate capitalism. A system not based on maximizing profits and growth for the few, but on adequate profit and sustainable growth for the good of all.

It is time to plant the seed in the womb of corporate capitalism and to nurture that seed. Jjust as an unhealthy mother can give birth to a healthy baby, we can use corporate capitalism to give birth to a new generation of capitalism – community capitalism.

What is community capitalism? It's an economy in which communities, as entities, use the tool of capitalism to acquire massive amounts of wealth, just as individuals and corporations have been doing for hundreds of years.

It's an economy in which communities, as investors, in partnership with existing businesses and entrepreneurs, own corporations. An economy in which community owned corporations seek only adequate profits and sustainable growth for the good of all.

I once met a person who was a licensed locksmith, but he liked to call himself a safecracker. The police sometimes would call him to open a safe that might have been associated with a crime. He was required to open it without doing any damage. No explosives, no cutting torches, just a bit of knowledge and human dexterity.

He told me that no matter how imposing the safe looked, he could open it because he knew enough about its internal mechanisms. In fact, he said, when manufacturers build safes, they do competent safecrackers the favor of building into the safe all the mechanisms necessary to crack it. If the doors were transparent, he said, it would be obvious how to open them to reveal the treasure inside.

So what's my point here? Simply this. Our economic system provides everything we need to build a new system that works for everyone. It provides everything we need to swing open the doors to the treasure inside. No bombs, no violence, no one to stand in the way to stop it. The treasure is there for the taking.

What is the treasure?

The treasure is a sustainable community that won't destroy the environment. A model in which:

- Communities not only are more powerful than corporations, they own corporations, too.

- People are more valued than profits. Where the economically powerful special interests are communities not corporate interests.

- Decentralized local economies are vibrant and controlled by local citizens, not by governments or municipalities. And are connected to other local economies around the nation and planet, for the purpose of helping each other. Unfettered by geopolitical boundaries.

- Small businesses flourish, and farmers are profitable, and children do not go to bed hungry!

- People have access to living-wage jobs, affordable housing, food, medical care, education, and time for their families, community life, and spiritual renewal.

This is the treasure we need to create a sustainable and hopeful future for all. If I had said this when I was young with little experience in these matters, I would have been told it is a utopian dream. Now that I am older with much more experience, I can say that this is no utopian dream.

This model can definitely be achieved. That is, if people want to do it. And it is time to do it now.

In fact, the model has it's already begun here in Western Massachusetts. This will be the first economy like the one we hope to form around the nation and the world. The road map to a new economic direction has now been drawn. The road to do this in Western Massachusetts has been completed. All of the necessary non-profit organizations, bylaws, policies, procedures, and other elements have been formed or been proven to be possible. In fact, there are already a few travelers walking the path.

Yet it is important to offer the Western Massachusetts prototype as a template for others around the nation and the world who are interested in creating a new economic reality for the common good.

The work to create the roadmap began in Easthampton at 11AM on the morning of January 1, 2000, the first day of millennium 2000. Because it was an economic model for the new millennium beginning 2000, I gave it a three-character Internet friendly designation E2M, meaning Economic Model for Millennium 2000.

Since then, one member became three, then eight, then twenty, and more. During the next seven years the pieces were steadily set in place. The model gained the support of educators, elected officials, entrepreneurs, labor leaders, individuals, and students.

The E2M model enables communities as entities to use the tool of capitalism to create enormous amounts of wealth. When communities have wealth they can invest with a new vision and create the shared economy and the world we need.

To create a shared economy, we can use the E2M model to establish decentralized regional economies that develop economic power by harnessing the purchasing power of the individuals living in the region. Just as a laser aligns very weak rays of light to produce beams powerful enough to vaporize metal, the E2M model aligns normally uncoordinated economic transactions to create a sustainable network of community controlled local economies that can usher us into a new era.

The E2M model requires neither new legislation nor the permission of any agency. This can all be done at the will of the people with practically no effort on their part. It doesn't require their time, which they don't have anyway. They do not need to donate money; which they don't have anyway. They just do the things they are already doing, but in a slightly different way.

It is the purpose of this book to explain exactly how we could do this. How we can create the new economic reality we are all hoping for. How we can create the shared economy and enter the next age.

Chapter 4 - It's About the Money

E2M allowed me to understand that many of the problems that we face in today's world – problems such as hunger, homelessness, poverty, violence in the family, the rise of inner city gangs, municipal insolvency, large-scale poor health, and more - come from one root cause. E2M also showed me that it is easier to eliminate the root cause than it is to eliminate any one of the many problems it causes; that is why I decided to make it my life's work to address the root cause. So on January 1, 2000, I wrote the first words of a document that would become a manifesto that essentially describes the problem and provides the solution. We simply need to fix the root cause.

Although there are many problems of diverse nature, it is my belief that the root cause of many of these problems is economic in nature. Thus E2M is economic in nature. It focuses only on the economic aspects of the current situation. We do not discuss specific problems in the social arena; we attack those problems from their root economic cause. E2M is about the money only. Once the economic problem is addressed, many other problems will evaporate. In the meantime, while we are addressing the economic problem, we can take some comfort that there are many organizations that already deal with other social problems. E2M does not need to duplicate their efforts; E2M is interested only in being an implementing force that provides fertile soil in which those other nonprofits and community-conscious organizations can flourish and succeed. It is the purpose of E2M to function on an economic level in order to enable communities to fund their transition into the shared economy to solve their own problems.

Some have suggested to me that E2M must also be about values, not just economics; however the idea of imposing values on potential E2M-member companies was rejected by the E2M.org board of directors after much discussion. Most important was that any entrepreneurs willing to join the E2M shared economy already possessed the most important value – giving to their employees and the community by sharing their wealth. As one myself, I know that entrepreneurs do not like being dictated to. Forcing values upon them could be placing obstacles to the operations of their companies and their entry into a shared economy. By establishing that shared economic system, we are more likely to create the power necessary to create broad economic, social, environmental, and cultural change that will instill those values.

There is a reason that the goal of E2M is to create a shared economy rather than to impose specific values on community-conscious entrepreneurs and their companies. That is because the most powerful system used to control or determine the direction of a society is the economic system; and we do not want to stand in the way of the creation of that shared economy.

Some might suggest that the political system is more powerful; however those who are in control of the economic system have the greatest sway over the political system. If we want to change our direction as a society, we must change the power structure within our economic system. This may sound daunting, but as you will learn, it is not. We can begin to achieve this goal anytime we want to start walking down the path.

Our current economic system was essentially created by relatively few, very wealthy people; thus it serves their interests rather the interests of the many. It is important to understand that just because the system seems to be all-encompassing, we do not have to accept it as our system if we are not happy with it.   Many of our most severe existing problems like hunger and poverty are artificial concepts thrust upon us by the current economic system. As a construct of humans, these concepts are subject to revision or replacement. And just as so many systems in the past have been replaced by more advanced and appropriate systems, so too we must develop a system that can achieve the society we need.

In the case of the current economic system, it is so entrenched, has such momentum, and is controlled by such powerful forces that it cannot be changed or even repaired. It is easier to move in a new direction than to try to fix something that is irreparable, not to mention unworthy of repair. The current system is mathematically unsustainable, and it will eventually unravel. It is a *Titanic* that is destined to sink. We can either stand on the deck and sing with the band, or we can launch the lifeboats and move in a new direction.

Fortunately, the power to decide when to launch is not in the hands of a few who are "in control"; that decision is in our hands. We, as communities, possess more power; we just do not exercise it because we are skeptical or we do not understand how to use our power. The order to launch can be issued by the common people anytime we want, and all who want to board are welcome, including the rich, but on our terms, not theirs. Either that or they can go down with their system. It's happened many times before in other countries.

Launching the lifeboats to move in a new direction does not mean that we are trying to replace or overthrow the current system. We are just creating a new direction and a new game with different rules for those of us who are disenfranchised with the current system and all its flaws. Stepping into the lifeboat is completely voluntary. To do so simply means we do not want to suffer the fate of the current system and those who rely on it. In fact, we will embrace the current system where we can by using the good things it offers. We will use its rules where they serve the greater good, but our goal and ultimate direction is different. Because our direction is voluntary, if you don't like what E2M suggests, you can stick with the old system and take your chances there. We force no one. We invite everyone.

Although we are not fighting with or against the current system, we must understand that change will not come from within that system. It will not evolve into the shared economy we seek; it is too corrupted and dysfunctional. True change comes from outside of the status quo, and we must create it ourselves if we are to achieve the future we want, rather than the future that those in power intend for us, that which benefits them most. They will not change their ways to suit us. We are on our own.

Some may not find this to be comforting because we have been taught that our government or the "system" is there to take care of us; but we have no choice if we are to create the future we want. Being on our own can feel unnerving, but that is the best way because when we are on our own, we can have it our way; we can have it any way we want.

Our direction is to a new future, a future without hunger, poverty, exploitation of the masses, economic chaos, and environmental degradation. It is within our grasp. It is ours for the taking. We can have it if we want it, and we can start right now.

If you want to build a ship, don't herd people together to collect wood and don't assign them tasks and work, but rather teach them to long for the endless immensity of the sea.

~Antoine de Saint-Exupery, French author and aviator

It's time for greatness – not for greed. It's a time for idealism – not ideology. It is a time not just for compassionate words, but compassionate action.

~Marian Wright Edelman, founder of
the Children's Defense Fund

Greatness is not in where we stand, but in what direction we are moving. We must sail sometimes with the wind and sometimes against it – but sail we must and not drift, nor lie at anchor.

~Oliver Wendell Holmes

Chapter 5 - The Root Cause

The root cause of many of our problems is that the goal for investment in the current economic system is to attain maximum profits and maximum growth for the benefit of relatively few investors and stockholders. Not only is this the dominant investment goal, it is also the purpose of the current economic system – to deliver profits based on continuous economic growth. Yet profitability is not enough; the goal is to maximize profits and growth. If there are profits this year, investors want more next year; enough is never enough! This is also the legal requirement and purpose of a corporation. This singular focus on maximizing profits and growth is the economic counterpart to unrestrained human greed.

Corporations must strive for this, or their stockholders can sue them.[1] Their only legal purpose is to maximize profit and growth regardless of the effect of their actions on the local community, society, or planet. This point is made clear in a Canadian-produced documentary titled 'The Corporation' which suggests that because corporations are legally considered to be "persons" and have the same legal rights as individuals, we should evaluate their "psychological make-up."

The filmmakers used the "diagnostic criteria of the World Health Organization, the standard diagnostic tool of psychiatrists and psychologists, to analyze the corporate psyche as one would a human being's."[2] It was shown that the "operational principles of the corporation give it a highly anti-social "personality": it is self-interested, inherently amoral, callous and deceitful; it breaches social and legal standards to

---

[1] https://h2o.law.harvard.edu/cases/3472
[2] http://www.thecorporation.com/index.cfm?page_id=312

get its way; it does not suffer from guilt, yet it can mimic the human qualities of empathy, caring and altruism."[3] If a human being possesses these same characteristics, that person meets the diagnostic criteria to be classified as a psychopath!

So when looking at large corporations, what we have are huge, multinational, psychopathic, economic organizations that will do anything they can to meet their goals of profitability and growth. Worse yet, these psychopathic behemoths have already begun to take control over our planet, the food chain, our political systems, and society in general.

Because the sole purpose of the corporation is to maximize profits and growth for its shareholders, corporations are expected to do anything they can to reach that goal regardless of the effect on society or the planet. A recent example of this is the case of the explosion of British Petroleum's Deepwater Horizon offshore drilling platform in the Gulf of Mexico. BP's corporate decisions to cut corners to save ten hours of time and ten million dollars in costs contributed to an explosion that has caused billions of dollars in damage, releasing almost 190,000,000 gallons of crude oil into the ocean[4]. This event destroyed the hopes and businesses of thousands of people, resulting in an unprecedented environmental catastrophe to the Gulf of Mexico and five U.S. states. Despite the fact that BP had just posted a six billion dollar profit as of March 30, 2010, managers just three weeks later on April 21st made catastrophic decisions to save $10 million, an amount equal to the profits made in less than four hours in the previous quarter.

---

[3] Ibid
[4] Campbell Robertson /Clifford Krauss (2 August 2010). "Gulf Spill Is the Largest of Its Kind, Scientists Say". The New York Times. New York Times. Retrieved 2 August 2010.

There are many other stories of corporate misbehavior and selfishness that could support the contentions of "The Corporation."

It is important to understand this characteristic of corporations for a very good reason. I believe the 25 years beginning in 2000 are the most important 25 years in the history of humanity. During that time, it will be determined who controls our planet – large psychopathic multi-national corporations seeking maximum profits wherever they can, or communities of people working together for the common good.

I think there is only one good choice, and that is communities. But how do we ensure that communities will be in control against the will of such huge and powerful corporate behemoths?

It will not be as hard as you think!

The... 20th century has been characterized by three developments of great political importance: The growth of democracy, the growth of corporate power, and the growth of corporate propaganda as a means of protecting corporate power against democracy.
~Alex Carey, Australian social scientist

We must rapidly begin the shift from a "thing-oriented" society to a "person-oriented" society. When machines and computers, profit motives and property rights are considered more important than people, the giant triplets of racism, materialism, and militarism are incapable of being conquered.　　　~Martin Luther King, Jr.

Chapter 6 – Maximum Profit and Growth

To understand how the will of the community can prevail over the will of the giant corporation, we need to get back to the issue of the maximization of profits and growth for relatively few stockholders. Why is the quest for perpetual maximization of profits and growth a serious problem? Let's just look at that for a moment to see how this greed-based paradigm threads itself throughout our social fabric to create enormous problems for millions of people.

This investment goal also encourages wealth acquisition strategies based on getting as much as you can as quickly as you can. And a lot of folks out there now are saying to themselves, I'd better get it while the getting's good, because things aren't going to get better; they're going to get a lot worse. This attitude is disturbing enough for the average person on the street, but it is now becoming the prevailing attitude of the financial elite whose investments determine the direction of our society, the economic health of millions of families, and the financial success of our nation.

Unfortunately, from the investor's point of view, maximum profits and maximum growth are not enough. If they achieved that this year, they want more next year. This goes on ad infinitum and ad nauseam. Enough is never enough for this group of people. Ask the former employees of any number of companies who got the pink slip because new owners of the company decided to shut it down because they could make more money by moving it elsewhere. The need to maximize profits affects not only employees and companies; it affects countries such as Asia in 1997 and 1998. In those years, investors and speculators removed huge amounts of investment capital from that region because they could get better returns elsewhere, thus thrusting that region into a major economic crisis. Whether it is an entire country or just one person, many hardworking people the world over have been tossed into the streets because relatively few investors wanted a bit more.

This max profit goal also calls for corporate missions that place profits before people. When corporations are required by investors to focus solely on maximizing profits and growth, they achieve it through a number of strategies. They can try to sell products for as much as they possibly can. Now competition, it is said, puts a damper on price inflation. However, as corporations merge and become larger, or purchase their competitors, or collude with them to keep prices stable, the price-stabilizing aspect of the competitive process diminishes. Many corporations become so large that smaller competitors simply cannot compete, even if they are selling the same product at a lower cost. The idea that competition keeps prices low does not necessarily hold water in today's world.

In addition to maximizing prices, corporations can minimize expenses to bolster profits. This calls for paying the lowest possible wages; eliminating benefits; busting unions; demanding maximum productivity from harried workers; outsourcing labor to China, India, and other countries; laying off employees at the first dip in profits; or using cheaper or poorer-quality raw materials. Just one example is recent headlines about contaminated paint on children's toys imported from China, or contaminated foodstuffs from foreign sources.[5] The news is endless yet the cause is the same. Cut expenses, increase profits. Poisoning people is part of the game.

---

[5] http://www.nytimes.com/2007/06/19/business/worldbusiness/19toys.html?pagewanted=all&_r=0

Another way that a corporation can be profitable is to purchase another corporation that is successful, that has sales, and that has a long-time workforce. They can buy that other corporation, pillage it for its assets, consolidate production facilities, lay off the workers, and keep only what they need – the sales and good assets. Any responsibility to pay liabilities oftentimes disappears in such "asset sales," and trade creditors receive pennies on the dollar. Such losses are passed on to the public in the form of higher prices to cover bad debt allowances. The takeover of existing successful and some unsuccessful companies can be one of the most effective ways to book profits and growth, other than, of course, outright Enron-style lying.[6]

To increase profits, corporations can also create new products, many of which are unnecessary and which exist only to make a profit. If there is no need for these new products, then advertisers will be hired to create the needs. And these advertisers will start as early as possible when parents place their two year olds in front of the television to keep them occupied. But it's not just kids they are after; as the rest of us sit glued to the tube, we are being sold something a good part of the time. Commercials tell us we're inadequate in some way– fat, ugly, uncool, growing a zit, not keeping up with the neighbors. Use this drug, grow more hair, have better sex, and on and on and on. This is advertising, psychological warfare at its best. They hire the brightest and most brilliant people to determine what they should say in their messages to make people buy.

This results in unsustainable rampant consumerization and consumption. Spend, spend, spend, buy, buy, buy. That is the over-arching message. These corporations must make money to satisfy their stockholders, and if that means producing junk

---

[6] http://www.nytimes.com/2006/05/25/business/25cnd-enron.html?pagewanted=all

to show a profit, then they will produce junk even if it's totally unnecessary. All this to keep you buying, to create more sales, to create more profits, to assure that the rich get richer, regardless of the amount of personal debt you take on. It is certainly true that we voluntarily subject ourselves to indebtedness by borrowing money or using credit cards to live beyond our means. However, the incessant forces of advertising we are exposed to beginning at very young ages are powerful enough to bring about cultural changes or to cause those less diligent or frugal individuals to succumb.[7]

As more and more products are produced, more and more raw materials are required, leading to resource shortages. And if we use them up in one location we'll just get them somewhere else, and use them up there, too. This can only go on for so long because we only have one planet and it has been shown that if all countries lived the same lifestyle as Americans, we would need three more planets the size of the Earth just to provide the resources.

All this excessive consumption creates more waste and pollution. Look at our massive landfills and polluted seas and atmosphere to see the end result. Along the same lines, more and more energy is required to produce and operate these new products, thus the need for more electricity and more power plants spewing an increasing amount of global warming CO_2.[8] Hence, rising global temperatures, melting ice caps, climate change, and environmental stress.

---

[7] The economic crisis which began in 2008 is causing many to rethink their lifestyles, make better buying decisions, and to re-examine their values, thus they are becoming less susceptible to the effect of the five thousand advertising messages they are exposed to daily.

[8] More recently we began fracking with its introduction of methane gas into water tables and the atmosphere. Methane is 27 times more powerful than CO_2 as a global warming gas.

The more energy we need, the more fossil fuels we use. As oil consumption increases, domestic resources diminish so we rely on oil producing nations who are not necessarily friends of America. We'll go anywhere we can to get our oil fix, and if we can't get it by negotiation, we can always consider taking it through force. As this goes on, the risk of resource wars increases. All for the purpose delivering more profits to investors who already have more money than they can ever spend!

The singular focus on profits also creates a culture of self-interest that pollutes the corporate, social, economic, and environmental agendas. You can't run a decent planet with everybody running around trying to make as much as they can as quickly as they can at the expense of everybody else. It's a dog-eat-dog world; it's the survival of the economically fittest; and it just doesn't work.

As the above scenarios expand and accelerate, there are other economic impacts on our society we need to be aware of. Of great concern is the fact that the goal of maximizing profit for a few stockholders results in inequitable concentration of wealth in our country and planet. Consider the following statistics:

In 2001, 1% of the entire American population owned almost 50% of all the private property in America. About 8% owned approximately 90% of all of the private property in America. The rest of us, the remaining 92% of the population, split the remaining 10% of assets, with a minority of these people owning a majority of what is left.[9]

---

[9] Gar Alperovitz, Boston Social Forum, July 2004. In 2016, political candidates tell us .1% owns more than 90% of the wealth!

In 2001, out of every 10,000 people in our population, 20 made more in stocks and bonds than the other 9,980 combined![10]

In 2001, of the $17 trillion of liquid investible capital, 1% of the population owned half, which equaled $8.5 trillion dollars. Another trillion dollars was owned by union pension funds, and the remaining $7.5 trillion by the population at large, again with the minority of them owning a majority of the remains. [11]

Let's look at this in another way. Have you ever played the game Monopoly when someone else has all the hotels, houses, utilities, and cash? You only have $50, Baltic Avenue, and are desperately trying to get to GO to collect your $200. And that's if you don't go to jail first! We all know how little fun that is. At least, you can take comfort in the fact that the game will end and you can start over with a clean slate.

Unfortunately the game I just described is the same game we are all playing in this current economic system. Every one of us, every baby born without a silver spoon in their mouth, is born into that economic game; and the deck is stacked against us.

That's why it is time to start a new game. A new game based on rules set out for the benefit of all rather than a game driven by greed using rules designed by the few to ensure they always win. What could the new game and rules look like and how can we begin to use it? You will have that answer in detail in the upcoming pages of this book.

---

[10] Ibid
[11] Ibid

An imbalance between rich and poor is the oldest and most fatal ailment of all republics.   ~Plato

Greed is a fat demon with a small mouth and whatever you feed it is never enough.
~Janwillem van de Wetering, Dutch novelist

Chapter 7 - Concentration of Wealth

As the statistics show, when you really look at the ownership and investment scenario in America, there is an extreme concentration of wealth. Much of this wealth is invested through six or seven investment companies. It is the stockbrokers and investment bankers in these companies who make the investments and trades that drive the stock market. They do it working hand-in-hand with each other, often over $150 lunches. Thus, the wealth concentrated in the top few percent of the populace is invested through even fewer people working in investment and brokerage firms doing what is best for themselves. This is not a healthy thing.

So let's look closer at this inequitable concentration of wealth. Why is it bad that the top one tenth of one percent (.1%) of the U.S. population owns as much wealth as the bottom 90%?[12] Well, it places economic power in the hands of the few. This is why many people now have lost faith in our government – they feel it is controlled by special interests, and I cannot disagree.

Money also attracts opportunities, so there becomes a concentration of opportunities. This is even more problematic than the concentration of wealth because it means that if you have an idea or if you want to try to get your piece of the dream, there are very few places to go for money now. It's very hard to get larger amounts of money, outside of the traditional investment world, so the best of new ideas and technologies are first offered to those who have enormous amounts of wealth or access to firms with wealthy investors. A

---

[12] http://inequality.org/wealth-inequality/

good example of this is when Facebook accepted significant amounts of investment capital from Goldman Sachs and a wealthy Russian investor well in advance of Facebook's IPO to the general public.[13] This is how wealth remains concentrated in the same hands generation after generation. Of course, since wealth can be inherited, the wealth gets passed along to descendants who happened to be born into it, further ensuring it remains in the hands of the same few.

Even more problematic is that as wealth in a society becomes more concentrated, it gives the few much more control over the masses through debt. The super-rich are the people who actually can afford to build and own massive amounts of property and assets. These assets include banks, corporate stockholdings, large tracts of land, commercial real estate, residential real estate, and massive amounts of consumer products such as appliances, automobiles, and other assets.

Because most of us cannot afford to buy our homes, cars, and appliances with cash, we use loans in the form of home mortgages, home equity loans, personal bank loans, and credit cards. Those loans increase the debt loads we acquire when borrowing from the super-rich through the banks they own. And until we pay every penny of it back to them, they have the legal right to foreclose on or repossess those items, even if we've paid most of it back. This happens in the courts through home foreclosures and even small claims lawsuits. If you are having a hard time and you are late on your mortgage payment even once, most mortgage contracts define that as a default and the bank can demand full payment of the loan at any time thereafter, even if you are back on schedule and the loan is current! If you don't pay them, they can institute foreclosure

---

[13] Since this chapter was first written in 2009, Facebook allowed Goldman Sachs and a Russian investor to purchase $500,000,000 of Facebook stock a year before the company went public. http://dealbook.nytimes.com/2011/01/02/goldman-invests-in-facebook-at-50-billion-valuation/

actions to take your house and put you on the street! This further subjugates the poor and the middle class who labor under poverty and excessive debt.

If you look at real income, it's going down while costs of living are going up. In today's world, two wage earners are required just to keep up. People work longer, harder, and faster for every dollar they can get. No wonder the American worker is the most productive of all countries. If they slow down, they'll be fired and put on the street. No wonder kids come back from school to empty homes and the family unit is breaking down. We don't sit around the dinner table any more. Some kids look to gangs to make up for the loss of family.

If there is only one parent, it's even more difficult. Stress levels, the "speed of society," and ill health are increasing. As our society begins to resemble a "survival of the fittest" reality show, people tend to become more cynical and self-serving. As the rich get richer, the middle class becomes poor, and the poor become homeless.

Finally, democracy suffers as special interests gradually take control and the populace becomes cynical and just stops voting. More people than ever now feel the government is not here to serve the people but rather to serve special interests and the rich.[14] As Supreme Court Justice Louis Brandeis said, "We can have a democratic society or we can have great wealth concentrated in the hands of a few. We cannot have both."

So, to summarize, we have a society in which most of the property is owned by relatively few people. The rest of us are in debt to those people; and as we buy more and more goods on credit, we increase the wealth of the rich while indebting ourselves even more. This results in increases in poverty,

---

[14] Gar Alperovitz, Boston Social Forum, July 2004.

homelessness, stress, ill health, and unhappiness. Cynicism grows, and people lose faith in their government, elected leaders, the economic system, and the future.

But don't lose faith; there is a solution! To appreciate how easy it is to implement the solution, we need to better understand the system in which all this is happening.

We must not allow ourselves to become like the system we oppose. ~Bishop Desmond Tutu

I regard class differences as contrary to justice and, in the last resort, based on force.
~ Albert Einstein

The most effective way to restrict democracy is to transfer decision-making from the public arena to unaccountable institutions: kings and princes, priestly castes, military juntas, party dictatorships, or modern corporations.
~Noam Chomsky, Linguist, Philosopher, Political Activist

Chapter 8 - The Current Economic System

Our economic system is a consumption-based system. That means it relies on continually increasing consumption of products and services to be considered healthy. Increases in consumption result in economic growth as measured by the Gross Domestic Product (GDP), the value of all goods and services produced in a year. When the economy grows, the investors who lend money to our government and businesses make a profit. The main purpose of our current economic system is to maximize profits and growth for these investors who are the driving force behind our economy. The more the economy grows, the more money these investors make. Thus, the goal of the economic system is to achieve growth. You know that because you now hear about economic growth all the time. It is the mantra of all politicians from the top down because it is good for investors, and investors make political contributions.

Although many people have investments, only a virtual handful of them possess most of the investible capital and private property in the U.S. In 2001 about eight percent of the U.S. population controlled close to half of all the private wealth in the U.S.[15]. Today less than one percent owns the vast majority of private wealth. If the economic system does not produce a profit for these relatively few investors, then they will take their money, as many are beginning to do, and send it to China or India and other places where they feel they can make more money. So in order for our economy to be successful, consumption must continually increase to keep the

---

[15] Gar Alperowitz, Boston Social Forum, July 2004

GDP growing so investors realize profits. But profits are not enough; investors want *maximum* profits and growth. If the GDP is $13 trillion dollars this year, investors want it to be more than that next year, and on and on.

If the GDP and consumption go down, we enter what's called an economic recession. So it's all about economic growth, and if the GDP is not growing, the investors will flee and the economy will crash. [16]

Okay, so we now understand that the economy must continually increase the production of goods and services and promote consumption. That is its mission. It lives for that. So who is it that purchases these goods and services? Its individual consumers like you and me. Our consumption of goods and services in America is responsible for 72% of the GDP. So out of the whole $13 trillion, the value of goods and services purchased by you and me is more than $9 trillion. This means that for our economy to be healthy, we need to keep buying. [17] If we stop buying there's no economic growth, the investors leave, and the economy tanks. Thus, consumer sales are the backbone of the U.S. and global economy. Economic stability requires that you and I purchase as much as possible. If we as consumers do the prudent and frugal thing, stop buying things we really don't need and start saving money, the economic system will collapse. [18]

---

[16] I first discussed this problem in 2001 and, as I predicted, the economy entered the Great Recession in September, 2008 when consumer confidence and purchases reached new lows. At that time scholars, Federal Reserve Chairman Alan Greenspan, and President Obama warned of possible global economic collapse.

[17] Our continued consumption is so important that immediately following the 9/11 attacks, President George Bush made it a point to tell the country to keep shopping. Time.com, 01/19/2009 Also https://www.youtube.com/watch?v=fxk9PW83VCY

[18] This was one of the causes of the economic collapse that began in September, 2008 when smart consumers just stopped buying due to personal fear, lack of confidence, and uncertainty.

This is nothing new. If we look back at historical facts, you can see what is happening to us.

Back in 1955, people were pretty much buying what they could afford with cash, although they did take home mortgages and car loans for their few major purchases. Individuals' cash and incomes were limited, and they lived a more frugal lifestyle, yet those investors who drive the economy wanted to make more money and that required more consumer sales. So what did they do? They said we've got to get these folks to buy more stuff, so let's create credit cards. So the credit cards came in and people began to mortgage their future. "Buy now, pay later" was the new slogan.

Then came corporate credit cards, home equity loans, second mortgages and third mortgages. As people went into further debt, spurred on by rampant consumerization of the society through television and other advertising, they began to increase their personal consumption. Even the government got in on the act by announcing tax rebates. Taxpayers received checks for $300 or so and went out to buy even more stuff. Thus the term "economic stimulus" was born to describe government give-aways.

Economic growth and expansion was the goal. To keep a healthy economy, we needed to expand economic growth. Thus we need to convince people to make more purchases because individuals' purchases are what drive economic growth. These purchases are the backbone of the economic system. In a 2001 speech about economic success, President Bill Clinton said, "The economy of the United States has expanded more in the years between 1985 and 2001 than it has in the history of America!" Let's look at Chart 1, below, graphing the years from 1955 to 2001. Note the height of the bars between 1955 and 1980 are fairly level while from 1985 to 2001, the period referenced by President Clinton, the increase from $2.1 trillion to $7.2 trillion is dramatic. Is this the chart of economic growth President Clinton was speaking about?

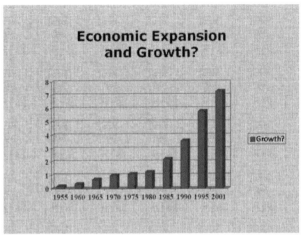

Chart 1

Unfortunately, this only *appears* to be a chart of the economic growth and expansion; it is not. It is a chart of U.S. household debt in trillions of dollars from 1955 to 2001!

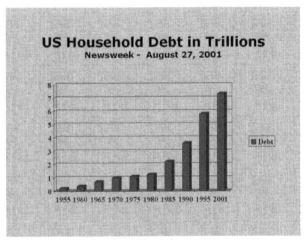

Chart 2

As you can see from Chart 2, above, essentially what happened was that at the same time that the economy was expanding at unprecedented rates, so too was total household debt!

You've seen what the Charts 1 and 2 look like for 1955 to 2001; now let's look at Chart 3 to see what happened between 2001 and 2005.

From 1985 to 2001 we jumped from about $2 trillion to $7.3 trillion in total household debt, an increase of $5.3 trillion in debt over 15 years. That's an average of about $350 billion per year.

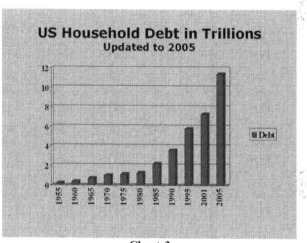

Chart 3

By 2005, total household debt was up to $11.4 trillion, an increase of $4.1 trillion in just in four years. That's an average of more than $1 trillion per year. That's three times faster! So, what's happening now is that we are increasing debt at a faster and faster rate. This is known as a hyperbolic curve; it gets steeper and steeper at an increasing rate. What this means is that the growth of household debt is out of control.

Look again at the curve in Chart 3. What's even more alarming is that although households took on huge amounts of debt between 2001 and 2005, it barely held the economy together and did not represent much of an improvement in people's lives. We took on all that debt just to keep the economy barely afloat. The economic system is so shaky that it requires even more and more consumption just to remain stable. It is much like a drug addict that requires more and more drugs just to feel good. Unfortunately, the drug addict is the current economic system and the few investors it serves, and the drug it requires is money– your money and my money. And as is true with drug addicts, the current economic system will do whatever it can to get its fix. We are coming to a point where there is going to be a major problem unless we, as citizens, stand up and do something about it.

One thing is certain; the problem is not going to take care of itself.[19] The government is not going to fix the problem; it is beholden to the few and it is of limited creativity. No great new political leader will have the cure, either.[20] The numerous scholars brought into government or with whom it has consulted have also failed to make any real headway as it relates to our current economic conditions. These people are not going to make a difference; the only people who are going to make a difference are those feeling the real pain.

You and I are the common people who feel the pain most when the current economic system falters; and we are the only ones with the motive to stand up for ourselves. Although there

---

[19] The debt situation came to a head in September 2008 when, due to loss of consumer confidence and criminal activity by Wall Street bankers, the U.S. economy collapsed and trillions of dollars of wealth was lost and bankruptcies soared. Total household debt went down temporarily, then rose to almost $12 trillion dollars in Q1 of 2015. http://www.businessinsider.com/ny-fed-q1-2015-household-debt-2015-5

[20] As I read this material for this edition, Vermont Senator Bernie Sanders has stepped to the plate as a candidate for the 2016 presidency, and he is creating a groundswell movement among the young. It will be a very interesting year!

are good reasons for us to feel we are victims of an outdated system, it is important to understand that although we may feel that way, and it may look that way, and even be that way, it is absolutely unnecessary that it remain that way.

History has shown that some of the most courageous people who have made great differences, either as individuals or communities, experienced some level of victimhood at some point. That victimhood is the catalyst that leads to great changes against very significant odds. Fortunately we do not face insurmountable odds because the hand of the people is the hand that can open the door to a shared economy and new era. Most exciting is the fact that opening the door does not require everyone; a small fraction of us is enough. As we establish the shared economy, the seeds we plant will grow and replicate as the door continues to open and cast a new light on great new possibilities.

As more and more people join us, we will have our shared economy. The time to open that door has arrived, and we must do it now before we lose the freedom to do it at all.

The shared economy is ours for the taking.

None are so hopelessly enslaved as those who falsely believe they are free.

~Johann Wolfgang von Goethe, German scientist

True individual freedom cannot exist without economic security and independence.

~Franklin D. Roosevelt

Without self-knowledge, without understanding the working and functions of his machine, man cannot be free, he cannot govern himself and he will always remain a slave.

~G. I. Gurdjieff, Greek-Armenian mystic and spiritual teacher

Chapter 9 - Is This Sustainable?

At lectures back in 2001 when I first began delivering this information, I asked members of the audience if anyone thought our economic system is sustainable. Can this go on?[21]

Most people agreed that the economy is not sustainable, it's a paper economy built on debt. So, if we agree that this is not sustainable, then we need to understand that it will eventually end, I would say, and we must ask ourselves the question When it ends, how does it end? What will that ending look like? Some people would say, an economic crash, others say social unrest or revolution. A few say the government will start a war. And more than one has said, I don't care, I'll be dead by then. So I ask you, my reader, the same question. Is this sustainable and if not how does it end? Today's news gives us more hints about what is to come of this.

The point I have been making since 2001 is that any system that requires continual increases in consumption and spending, and which continually increases the indebtedness of the populace in order to be considered healthy and to survive, cannot survive indefinitely. Consumers will eventually be

---

[21] It did not go on. In September 2008, seven years after this lecture, the economy began a collapse that was the most severe since the Great Depression. Consumers became so over-indebted that they just stopped buying and started to save money, which is exactly the right thing for an indebted person to do. But what is good for people is not good for investors so something had to be done to make up for the loss of consumer spending. That began the most expansive government spending program in the history of America. A total of $13 trillion of taxpayer money was provided to bail out banks and investors while millions of families lost homes through foreclosure. Federal Reserve Chairmen Greenspan and Bernanke said they were surprised and never saw it coming! But this farm boy from Massachusetts predicted it in written documents years earlier! Something doesn't sound right here. Chairman Bernanke says the worst is over and we'll see a return to a healthy economy. This farm boy doesn't agree. I believe this is just the part where our Titanic economy hits the iceberg. There is more to come.

driven into such levels of debt that they will stop buying things they don't really need and decide to live a simpler life. This was proved in September 2008 when consumers stopped consuming. At the same time, it become obvious those bankers, investment houses, and other schemers had been up to no good by violating the public trust using unethical and immoral financial machinations to enrich themselves while nearly collapsing the global economy.

The fact is clear now that if overly indebted consumers stop spending, somebody, anybody, needs to spend lots of money or the system is going to collapse. So in order to keep the system alive, the government and Federal Reserve System had to step in with the Economic Stimulus package of 2008 and spent more than $10 trillion of public monies to bail out banks and their investors, and thus prevent economic chaos and collapse.[22] That might have worked once, but the backlash to Presidents Bush, Obama, and numerous other politicians were so severe that there is no appetite for another economic rescue package. This is especially true considering that the government spending that took place used taxpayers money; and that is money you, your children, and I will be paying for years to come. The bottom line is that if the current economic system can't deliver profits to investors by getting the money out of your wallets voluntarily, the government will give the investors their profits directly by funding bailouts and bonuses then take it out of your pocket in taxes. No matter what, it's going to come out of you and me unless we decide to stand up for ourselves and break the bonds that limit our individual prosperity.

More astounding yet is the fact that our duly elected government gave our money to these same bankers and

[22] http://www.nytimes.com/interactive/2009/02/04/business/20090205-bailout-totals-graphic.html

investment companies who pander to super rich banks and investors. Yet these same bankers refuse to provide audits on how that money was spent or to provide any financial relief for millions of homeowners who were deceived into taking mortgages they couldn't afford. Instead the bankers continue their practices of paying themselves billions in bonuses; foreclosing on our homes in the name of these investors; and charging us more than $38 billion a year in credit card late fees, checking account overdraft charges, inactivity fees, and anything else they can conjure up to feed themselves an unending stream of money at our expense. Are you getting fed up with this yet? Are you ready to take back your life? Perhaps it is time for you to decide.

Our society is on a treadmill of ever-increasing speed. As we work harder for less, we are consuming more natural resources and creating more pollution and waste to make more and more products, many of which are unnecessary. All the while, we are increasing climate change and risking the health of our air, seas, and planet. As Mohandas Gandhi once said, "There is more to life than increasing its speed."

So what we need to do is to somehow throttle this situation back because it's a self-perpetuating machine that doesn't know how to stop itself. It will continue on its irrational path until it just blows up. And even the rich are victims; it will just take them longer to realize it. They too will be at risk if our society becomes seriously dysfunctional. Even U.S. history has shown what happens when people reach a state of hopelessness. We saw that in the 1960s. We saw that as cities burned around the country, brought on by anger and hopelessness in many African-American communities. Today, disenchantment is growing in white communities in America, among the young in France, and more recently in Malaysia, Thailand, Greece, and in other areas. When people reach a state of hopelessness, the unimaginable becomes reality. You may not be ready to believe this, but your elected officials aren't so dismissive of the possibility.

I have to point out also that the changes in personal privacy, the Patriot Act, loss of habeas corpus, warrantless wiretaps, all these things that our government has done to protect America from foreign terrorists, can all be waged in response to a massive economic collapse. At times like this, normally law-abiding citizens who just can't handle it anymore go to the streets as has happened before. It is not an impossibility even in America, and many are already preparing for it. Fortunately it does not have to go that far; there is a peaceful solution and the choice is ours.

Washing one's hands of the conflict between the powerful and the powerless means to side with the powerful, not to be neutral.
 ~ Paulo Freire, Brazilian educator and theorist

They who would give up an essential liberty for temporary security, deserve neither liberty or security.
 ~Benjamin Franklin

As nightfall does not come all at once, neither does oppression. In both instances, there is a twilight when everything remains seemingly unchanged. And it is in such twilight that we all must be aware of change in the air however slight, lest we become unwitting victims of the darkness.
 ~Supreme Court Justice William O. Douglas

Chapter 10 – What's the Solution?

So, what's the solution? Do we dismantle the system? I have heard that "solution" from people who are anarchists. They want to tear the system apart. But I can tell you, it is not likely that anyone is going to dismantle the system. Look here. This is a picture of the Sunday, May 2, 1971 *Washington Post* reporting on a massive demonstration when 250,000 young people went to Washington to shut the government down.

It says, 'The camped protesters, with the setting sun in the background, listened to a rock concert.'

This civil action was about civil rights; it was about the war. Young folks had had enough; their position was that "We've been trying to end this war nonviolently and you're not listening to us so we're going to come down and we're going to shut Washington down." That was Sunday, May 2, 1971.

This is Tuesday, May 4, 1971:

It reads, '7,000 Arrested Disrupting City.'

That was the largest number of private citizens ever arrested by the U.S. government in the history of America. The caption under the picture says: 'Troops make a helicopter landing on the Washington Monument grounds. In all some 180 soldiers landed there. Few demonstrators were in the vicinity of the monument at the time and no confrontations took place.'

I happened to be one of those few, and as I stood there watching a military war machine deploying armed troops while landing on an iconic Washington Monument lawn, I remember thinking "Now we've got their attention!" However, my own freedom was short-lived when I was arrested along with another 4,000 young people during the next three days.

When the citizenry marches on the government with the purpose of demanding that it account for its actions or even to replace them, the government is not going to take it lying down. The government will respond militarily, as seen in this picture of a military Huey helicopter landing on the lawn of a national monument deploying soldiers carrying automatic rifles with fixed bayonets.

So let me tell you, the helicopters are now better, the soldiers better trained, and the weapons more sophisticated than in 1971. Shutting down the system is not the way to do it. It's not going to happen. It's not the way to go.

Another option might be to change the laws? That's not too likely. Changing the laws takes too long and there's not enough political will or citizen power to do it. The system is dedicated to maintaining the status quo and the special interests are too powerful. Hell, the government backed down when rich bankers, investment houses, and corporations refused to provide audits on what they did with the trillions they stole from the people. So trying to get legislative action to create an economy of the people and by the people is not going to happen. If it could, it would have happened long ago before this mess got as bad as it is.[23] But there is a way.

This economic system we are in lives to keep the current investors happy. It is these relatively few members of society who own the vast majority of assets and who are major stockholders in corporations, banks, and investment houses

---

[23] In July of 2009, a very popular President Barack Obama tried to forward the idea of using some of the TARP bailout funds to relieve the pressure on millions of citizens facing home foreclosure. The legislation failed because Congress felt it was not in the best interest of investors.

who are creating the problem. These stockholders or their investment managers have insatiable appetites and do not know when enough is enough. They are the unnamed and invisible investors who ultimately preside over corporate managers who are required to deliver maximum profits and growth. If corporate managers do not deliver the goods as indicated by quarterly profit and loss statements, these stockholders can and will demand their resignations. So in a sense, even corporate managers are victims.

These managers are our neighbors. They leave home in the morning, hug their wives and children, care about their neighbors, and are much like you and me. But when they get to the office in the corporate culture, they must march to a different tune. There, it is all about the money, and if they don't deliver, they'll be put on the street in a New York second. They'll do whatever is necessary to maximize the bottom line, whether it means laying off 50 people or even 5,000, or it means ignoring any negative impacts they make on society, or damaging the environment. It doesn't matter; when you cross the threshold in today's corporate culture, you are often required to check your humanity at the front door, preferably outside the front door, all to ensure you maximize profits and growth for a group of invisible investors. So ultimately, it is the investors, driven by human greed, who are a major part of the problem.

So what we need to do is change the investors or stockholders. We need to find investors who do not demand maximum profits and maximum growth from their investments. We need investors who will accept a new investment goal of adequate profit, sustainable growth for the good of all. This is a goal that is not based on greed or a singular focus on profits. This is a more humane and sustainable goal that says it's okay to make less if it will create a sustainable society for the common good. In fact, this new goal is the basis for a new free-market, capital-based, economic system I refer to as E2M. It is a "common good economy" based on "common good economics." It is a shared economic system that accepts that enough is enough. It's mission includes caring, sharing, watching out for our fellow beings and planet, and throttling back the speed of society to a more manageable and sustainable level.

In a sustainable E2M shared economy, adequate profit could be 1% a year; and sustainable growth could even be zero growth at times. And for the good of all? Well, getting investors to accept that is the hardest part. Not only do we need to find investors that will accept these new criteria, these investors must be ever-present and unwavering. They can't change their minds; once they're in, they have to stay in for the long haul. And they must have access to very large amounts of funding. We will need more than a few million dollars; we need billions available for investment under this new criterion.

So where can we get this money? Who would accept this new goal for investment? Small-time investors like you and me? Well, I think we are so far in debt that we need to profit as much as possible from our limited investments.

How about philanthropists? No, not them either. There aren't enough of them, and they can change their minds at any time. To succeed, this investment goal must be woven throughout the fabric of society, never to be unraveled.

But don't despair, the good news is that there is such an investor, an investor that will not only accept adequate profit and sustainable growth for the good of all, but who *must* achieve it or this investor will die. And this investor has access not to millions or even billions of dollars; this investor has access to trillions of dollars. Do you have an idea of who this investor might be?

"The government?" some people ask. No it is not the government; it is too focused on pleasing very wealthy special interests that are causing the problem.

This new investor is the community itself. It is we, as a community, who spend trillions of dollars a year. We can become that new investor. We spend an enormous amount of money every year. Although, as individuals, we are not as economically powerful as that small group of super-wealthy individuals, we are hugely powerful as a group. We just aren't as organized as they are, but that is possible to change.

We are the ones who make the rich wealthy by purchasing more than $10 trillion dollars of products and services a year from companies owned primarily by the very wealthy few. Much of it is purchased by incurring some form of debt that will take us years to pay off. Almost all the money possessed by them came from us, as a community, in the first place.[24] In essence, as we buy from them and increase their wealth, we are increasing their power to lord over us! It's like chickens feeding the foxes who are eating them!

If we, as regional communities, could create vast pools of citizen-controlled community wealth, we could invest it with a new vision based on achieving adequate profits and sustainable growth for the good of all.

---

[24] More recently the U.S. government and the Federal Reserve committed almost $13 trillion dollars to bail out banks and to pay huge bonuses to the same bankers who knowingly made unsound investments to turn huge profits. More billions went to bail out investment houses, automobile manufacturers, and other large corporations owned by the super rich in America and foreign countries. As usual, all this money will come from you, me, our children and grandchildren in the form of taxes, new banking fees, as well as higher interest rates. Maybe its time for us to stand up for ourselves. - MG

This investment goal is the economic foundation of the shared economy. We only need to produce enough community wealth to begin our journey to establish a new future and enter a new economic era that works for everyone!

Those who make peaceful revolution impossible will make violent revolution inevitable.

~John F. Kennedy

Intelligent discontent is the mainspring of civilization. Progress is born of agitation. It is agitation or stagnation.

~Eugene V. Debs, Union leader and Indiana State Senator, 1880

Chapter 11 - Creating Community Wealth

The key to creating a new world for the many, rather than for the few, is for us to harness our community wealth in a way that can usher in a shared economy based not on greed, avarice, and injustice, but on sharing, caring, and yes, love. Because so much of life is about the money, it is high time for us, as a community, to take control of our economic decisions to create as much community-controlled wealth and economic power as possible. The more community wealth we can assemble for our own purposes, the quicker we can establish the shared economy and new era.

So how are we to acquire this wealth? Take it from the rich? Some would say so, but that is not likely and would take too much effort in any event. The solution is much easier than to "take it from the rich."

Can we create it through taxes? Not likely for the same reasons. Besides, we are already overtaxed and our elected officials are very resistant to assessing even more taxes. If any new taxes are assessed, they will be used to fund the financial bailouts of rich bankers and investment houses, not to create a free and independent economic system by, of, and for the people.

The way to create this community wealth is the same way most other people and corporations create vast wealth, they earned it! We, as communities could do the same thing, earn it, if we just had a mechanism to do that.

This is exactly what the E2M economic system does. E2M creates the infrastructure that enables the community to create enormous amounts of community controlled wealth using the most powerful tool known in the history of humanity to create wealth. That would be the tool of capitalism!

Just as a laser aligns normally weak rays of light into beams that can vaporize metal, E2M enables communities to coordinate millions of economic transactions into streams of community wealth and capital powerful enough to change the world and usher in a new era that could last for millennia.

E2M enables the community, as an entity, to use the tool of capitalism to create as much wealth for itself as it wants, not by taxing it or taking it away from the rich, but by earning it, just as individuals and corporations have been doing for centuries. And when the community picks up the same tool of capitalism that has enriched and empowered individuals and corporations for centuries, the community can become a formidable competitor.

Using the E2M model, communities can create as much wealth as they want, at will, and become more economically powerful than the largest corporations. As communities begin growing their wealth, they can invest it in a manner that serves the collective good—just as is done by philanthropists, benevolent organizations such as the United Way and other foundations, nonprofit corporations and some socially responsible investment firms.

Just imagine what we can do with enormous amounts of community-controlled wealth to provide solutions to social issues. Take homelessness for one example. We could use community wealth to build affordable houses, apartment buildings, or inner-city condominiums, making them available to community members by providing 50-year mortgages at a one percent interest rate. So instead of a $200,000 house costing $1220 per month at 6% interest over 30 years, that same house would cost $423 a month, a savings of $800 per month. A $50,000 inner-city condo would cost less than $25 per week. We can eliminate homelessness at these rates! Better yet, let's purchase foreclosed homes from banks for pennies on the dollar and refinance them to their former owners over 50 years at 1% interest and solve the foreclosure crisis once and for all! The main obstacle between the homeless and homes is the interest rates charged by banks trying to maximize their profits.

With community-controlled wealth, the community could work with entrepreneurs to help them start new companies. As a venture investor in these companies, communities could be entrepreneur-friendly partners.

In the current economic system, an ideal venture capitalist-type investment would be to provide a new company with $2 to $3 million; grow that company to $100 million in sales within three to five years; then in seven years or so, sell it out to a "strategic partner," which really means a major corporation, so that the venture investors can earn $20 or $30 million on their $2 to $3 million dollar investment. When the new strategic partner takes over, they often sell off all the excess assets or machinery, close down duplicate office locations, lay off everybody that operated those machines or worked in those offices, then move the operation out of town to one of their other locations or to a city that will give them huge tax breaks to get the jobs the company will bring. That's the venture capital approach to investing.

The community as an entrepreneur and employee-friendly investor could help start companies with the much more humane understanding that the new company need not be a multi-million dollar corporation invested in for the purpose of flipping as soon as possible as demanded by venture capitalists. The community would be happy to help entrepreneurs start a good company, create a good product and grow sustainably as a local business employing local people. That, of course, does not prevent companies from doing well and growing fast; it just doesn't demand maximum growth and profits in return for the investment. In fact, once communities and entrepreneurs work together to form these companies, community members can support them by purchasing their products, thus guaranteeing the success of the company, the entrepreneur, the employees, and the community.

Using their wealth, communities could prevent the gentrification caused by real estate speculation and gouging. This is exactly what happened when I received an urban blight grant at the Valley Community Development Corporation in Western Mass. In 2001, I received a community development grant and rented a storefront office for $5 a square foot in the blighted downtown business district of Easthampton, Mass. where there was a 40% vacancy rate caused by the departure or failure of the city's manufacturing businesses. During the next 30 months, my office helped low-income folks start 26 new businesses that filled all the empty spaces. The newspapers ran many stories about these new companies and my office began hearing from many more budding entrepreneurs. The situation became known as the "Easthampton Renaissance." Once the storefronts were filled, however, real estate speculators began to buy up commercial properties and rents doubled.

In a nearby community, rents were $4 to $5 a square foot in 1980 and had risen to $40 a square foot by 2002 as that city became a tourist destination. A good number of small businesses couldn't afford to remain there and either moved or closed as national chains moved in. The success of these new small local businesses began to work against them as their leases expired and rents were increased.

Community wealth could be used to purchase commercial buildings in downtown centers, provide space for small businesses, then keep the rent stable for years. This could occur because communities aren't in the business of making as much money as possible from small businesses; they are in the business of keeping small businesses healthy, which also contributes to the long-term health of the community. This would be a wonderful alternative to the current situation in which the success of small businesses can work against them as they succeed and make city centers more attractive, thus driving up rental rates.

These are just a few examples of the huge positive power of community wealth invested with the goal of adequate profit and sustainable growth for the common good. This is something rarely achieved or even desired by private investors who are primarily acting in their own individual self-interests. Let's face it; all humans have an element of self-interest and greed. We're not going to change that; that's the way it is. So that's why we need to create community wealth where we can all get into the room together and think about how much good we can do. That is exactly what the E2M economic model does. By gathering as a group, citizens can think and invest collectively for the common good and overcome the need to achieve the returns they need to make as individual investors. That is how we avoid the limitations of greed-based investment strategies and replace them with investment strategies driven by benevolence – to serve the greater good.

It might be obvious to you by now that the current consumption-and-growth-based economic system with a singular focus on profits and growth is unsustainable and headed for a major "unraveling." A more caring, sharing system based on sustainability and the common good is necessary if we are ever to stop the madness we see around us and create long-term sustainability and success as a human race.

We cannot fix the current system; it is unsustainable, broken, and subject to collapse. It is easier to move in a new direction to bring about the positive change necessary to open the doors to a shared economy that works for everyone.

Let's explore some possibilities.

Capital as such is not evil; it is its wrong use that is evil. Capital in some form or other will always be needed.
~Mohandas K. Gandhi

Small opportunities are often the beginning of great enterprises.

~ Demosthenes, Greek statesman and orator, 384-322 B.C.

Chapter 12 - How the E2M Economic Model Works

The E2M economic model is an alternative to the current unsustainable economic system that is causing so many problems. E2M is designed to be a global network of decentralized regional shared economies that exist to provide a sustainable and equitable society for all people. The regional shared economies are chartered into existence by E2M.org, yet are largely independent of E2M.org and of each other. If necessary, they may act collectively using E2M.org as a facilitator. As a network of independent but collaborative regional shared economies, the regions would be members of a national E2M council. These national councils would also become members of a global E2M Congress representing different countries. The national and international organizations exist primarily to facilitate communications, transactions, and initiatives between the most important elements of the E2M economic network, the regional economic communities. So let's look at what they are all about.

An E2M regional shared economy has three components: an E2M Regional Economic Council, a number of E2M-affiliated businesses, and the residents of the region, also referred to as the Community.

The E2M Regional Economic Councils (E2M-REC): These are councils populated and controlled by community members. The E2M-RECs are nonprofit organizations whose mission is to represent the best interests of the regional community. They are chartered by E2M.org and are authorized to hold the community's wealth and use that wealth to benefit the community. They can enter into business transactions, hold corporate equity, receive and disburse funds, start businesses, invest in businesses, launch social initiatives, and engage in other community-building activities.

E2M-Affiliated Businesses: These are businesses of all kinds—corporations, sole proprietorships, partnerships, cooperatives, foundations, nonprofit organizations, and others—that have chosen to join the local E2M regional shared economy. For-profit businesses donate a portion of their equity and/or income to the E2M-REC and may have profit-sharing plans for their employees. Non-profits pay a small fee.

The Community: This is the general public that resides in the area encompassed by the E2M regional shared economy. The general public spends very significant amounts of money on goods and services. By purchasing those goods and services from E2M-affiliated businesses, or by purchasing E2M-branded products, community members can guarantee that these businesses will grow and provide a significant and steady flow of wealth to the E2M Regional Economic Councils to benefit the local region. This wealth is used to create a truly healthy community and invest in or start up more E2M-affiliated businesses, which also donate funds and equity to the E2M Regional Economic Council. Thus consumers can support E2M-affiliated or E2M community-owned businesses and products to create the wealth communities need to transform our society.

Everyone wins with E2M—the community, the owners of E2M companies, their employees, and the people who invest in these companies.

Because E2M is dedicated to creating an economy for the common good, I am occasionally told that E2M "sounds like socialism." This is totally unfounded because in a socialist system, the state is ultimately the overseer of the economy. It is a system whereby the state feels it can do a better job of providing for the populace than the populace can for themselves.

E2M, in fact, more closely resembles capitalism in its purest form as intended by Adam Smith, the father of capitalism. Smith's intention was for all social sectors to be economically healthy, i.e., the land baron, the entrepreneur, and the peasant worker. He felt that if people acted in their own self-interests, an "invisible hand" would become the guide to economic justice for all. He expounds on this in more detail in his books *The Theory of Moral Sentiments* and *The Wealth of Nations* published in 1759 and 1776, respectively.[25]

Smith's theories may have been valid in the years before the Industrial Age; however, due to a number of factors relating to the increases in human productivity brought on by industrialization, his hoped for outcomes were not ultimately realized. He abhorred the idea of monopolies and would probably frown on the current economic system because he was strongly opposed to concentrations of economic power that could interfere with the natural operation of his economic system.

Similar to a capitalist system, which allows individuals and corporations to act in a manner that best serves their own self-interests, E2M is simply a free-market economic model that enables communities to participate in economic activity that ensures their own self-interests. For this reason, E2M has been called "community capitalism," "community conscious

---

[25] "The Life of Adam Smith," John Rae, 1895, Macmillan and Co.

capitalism," a "shared economy," and a "common good economy."

Thus, E2M is a free-market system that enables communities, as entities, to participate independently and freely in the economic process to produce community wealth in order to take care of themselves without any over-lording by a socialist or even a democratic government.

I believe Adam Smith would approve of E2M for its ability to achieve his original goals while overcoming the negative effects on society brought on by the current economic system, which is a distortion of Smith's idea of capitalism.

Apathy can be overcome by enthusiasm, and enthusiasm can only be aroused by two things: first, an ideal, which takes the imagination by storm, and second, a definite intelligible plan for carrying that ideal into practice.

~Arnold Toynbee, British economic historian

Chapter 13 - The Three Pillars of an E2M Regional Shared Economy

Because the E2M regional shared economy stands firmly on three important pillars, it is important that we look at them in more detail and understand how they interact with each other. As you know, the three pillars are the members of the general public who comprise the Community, the E2M Regional Economic Council, and E2M-affiliated businesses. The diagram below shows the relationships between these three main elements of the E2M regional shared economy

An E2M Economic Community

Let's look at these three components in more detail.

E2M Regional Economic Council:

The E2M Regional Economic Councils use the community's wealth to benefit the common good of the community. It is a nonprofit organization of local citizens that is demographically representative of the regional community in which it is being formed. These demographics include gender, age, race, religious affiliations, sexual orientation, and economic status. This is to ensure a representative council that is fair to all and respected by community members. This would avoid the problems caused by an all-white council in a primarily African-American population or a Christian council in a Muslim community. Although this might seem discriminatory, it is actually representative to avoid such situations as experienced in a formerly apartheid South Africa, religiously separated Ireland, or pre-Civil Rights Act America. Council members are pastors, educators, entrepreneurs, laborers, rich and poor. They will convene monthly in open meetings to address community issues and receive input from community members. Subcommittees would be formed to provide advice on finances, social issues, and other matters a demographically representative council may need. The procedure to establish an E2M Regional Economic Council is straightforward and accessible to any interested group:

1. Eight citizens must petition E2M.org to start an E2M regional shared economy in their region. As the chartering organization for new regions, E2M.org will evaluate the petitioning group. Once the petitioners receive their charter to form a new E2M Regional Economic Council, they will follow a specific procedure to increase the Council's size:

2. The original eight individuals will populate the E2M Regional Economic Council for the first year.

3. During the second year, eight new members are nominated by members of the local community and elected to the E2M Regional Economic Council by its current members, bringing the total membership to 16 people.

4. An additional eight individuals are added during the third year, bringing the total membership to 24.

5. Starting in the fourth year, eight new members are added while the oldest sitting eight are retired. Retiring members may be re-nominated for membership to the E2M Regional Economic Council; however, no board member may serve more than two concurrent terms. These term limits are designed to ensure that there are no concentrations of power within the board.

6. Any board member is subject to dismissal at any time by a democratic process of removal. This process may vary from region to region as suggested by each local E2M Regional Economic Council and approved by the E2M.org board before the charter is granted. If the E2M Regional Economic Council requesting an E2M Charter does not suggest the procedures for a democratic process of dismissal, E2M.org will provide a procedure.

7. E2M Regional Economic Councils will provide an annual financial report and self-evaluation to E2M.org, which will be available to the public.

The E2M Regional Economic Councils receive funds from E2M-affiliated businesses and from the sale of products created by E2M.org and sold in the general marketplace. When an affiliated business provides funds to the E2M Regional Economic Council, the employees of that business designate where half of that donation is spent.

The E2M Regional Economic Council spends the remainder of the donation such that 75% of its monies are spent locally for social, economic, environmental, or other community initiatives. Another twenty percent (20%) is to be spent nationally, with a considerable focus on helping to establish E2M Regional Economic Councils in other regions as part of a strategy to create a self-replicating system whose separate regions support and share with each other.

We're looking to create an economic network around this planet that is based on caring and sharing and working and trading with each other. Thus, the final 5% is to be spent internationally to promote that effort. Not that a $50 dollar check to a foreign land is going to make a big difference, but what that does is to create a line of communication and it's upon these initially tenuous lines of communication that the E2M-based shared economic system will grow. These initial relationships may lead to further communications, financial interactions, and business transactions in which goods flow as imports or exports between these regions. As a result of these relationships, the E2M regional shared economy and network will grow around the planet.

How the E2M Regional Economic Councils use their funds: Employees of E2M-affiliated companies will very likely choose to designate that 50% of their company contribution be spent for community investments and initiatives. Therefore each E2M Regional Economic Council will use about 70% of the remaining undesignated income to make financial investments in new or existing E2M-affiliated businesses.

By accumulating larger amounts of investible funds derived from the individual donations of existing E2M-affiliated companies, the E2M Regional Economic Councils can become an equity investor for new businesses.

As an equity investor contributing to new start-up businesses, the local E2M Regional Economic Council, as a nonprofit organization, will own up to 50% of that start-up company. As community members actively seek out and support these E2M start-up businesses and products, the E2M Regional Economic Council will receive greater returns and can use those funds to form even more E2M Certified businesses that will continue to increase the community's wealth and economic power. This power of leverage is extremely significant. The E2M Regional Economic Councils form companies and products that produce profits to create even more companies and products that can be actively supported by communities to develop the economic power to change the world. Using this leverage power, E2M Regional Economic Councils can make as much money as they want, as fast as they want, so long as community members support E2M-affiliated companies and products. Such products could include locally made foods, clothing, housewares, biofuels, renewable energy providers, and more. It is very easy for the members of the community to identify these companies and products because they all display the tri-spiral E2M logo you see at the beginning of each chapter in this book.

It is important to understand that as an investor in E2M-certified businesses, the E2M Regional Economic Councils will not expect these businesses to produce *maximum* profits and growth. Instead, they will accept adequate profits and sustainable growth—enough profit for the business to continue providing high-quality, truly useful products and services to the community while creating stable, living-wage jobs, returns for entrepreneurs running the companyE2M-affiliated and its investors, while keeping its resource consumption and pollution to a minimum.

In its capacity as a venture investor, the E2M Regional Economic Councils will seek out entrepreneurs who want to start E2M-affiliated businesses or E2M-branded product lines.

The E2M Regional Economic Councils would announce their intention to start a business and identify entrepreneurs who want to file an application to be a part of it. Simply stated, an ad for the position might read, "We seek entrepreneurs to lead a start-up business. You will have a piece of equity; the employees are going to have a piece of equity; and you're going to get a paycheck every week. Numerous consumers are waiting to purchase the products of this business. Possibility for success is extremely high." Many entrepreneurs would be happy to take that deal based on the fact that a significant number of start-up businesses fail within several years.

E2M-affiliated businesses

If the E2M Regional Economic Council is to create community wealth, we need a way to gather it. We are not going to gather it from taxes because only the government has the authority to tax, and most people are already overtaxed. We are not going to take it from the rich; it's theirs. What we intend to do is to gather wealth the way individuals and corporations have been doing it for hundreds of years; we are going to earn it. We are going to earn it using the most powerful tool in the history of humanity for gathering and concentrating wealth, the tool of capitalism in a free-market system.

In such a free-market economy, dollars flow in many directions in numerous income streams that range from smaller cash flows to massive amounts of money. The entities that gather monies from these continually flowing streams, the entities that are the magnets for wealth, are corporations. So if the community is to gather wealth from the economic system, it needs to have a relationship with corporations to help earn the monies that will build community wealth. Thus, another component of the E2M regional shared economy is the E2M-affiliated corporation or business.

This is a business that is run, owned or developed by a new breed of entrepreneurs. They may be younger folks who have a commitment to use their businesses for a higher purpose, or older folks like me who've already had a business, do not accept the traditional ideas that place a singular focus on profits, and who have come to the conclusion that there must be a better way to operate a business.

E2M-affiliated businesses could be businesses of all types—corporations, limited liability companies, professional companies, sole proprietorships, partnerships, cooperatives, foundations, nonprofits, and others that have chosen to participate in E2M in one of three different ways:

1.) An **E2M Gold Logo company** donates at least one half of a percent (.5%) of its total sales and a minimum of 5% of its stock or equity to the community through the E2M Regional Economic Councils. In addition, it sets aside a minimum of 5% of its profits for employee profit-sharing plans and 5% of its equity in stock option plans for its employees. The remaining 90% of equity and profits belong to the company's owners and investors. This is the Gold Level of participation.

2.) An **E2M Silver Logo company** is a business that donates at least one half of a percent (.5%) of its total sales income to the community through the E2M Regional Economic Councils. This is the Silver Level of participation.

3.) An **E2M Bronze Logo company** is a business that donates at least one half of a percent (.5%) of its sales income from a particular product line or service that the business offers. It is encouraged that E2M Bronze Logo companies donate a larger percentage of income as sales resulting from E2M-affiliation grow or even become a significant part of total sales. This is the Bronze Level of participation.

Of the money that is contributed to the E2M Regional Economic Councils by these companies, one-half will go to causes designated by a vote of the owners and employees of that company. This will enable all members of the company, regardless of rank, to decide how to contribute to the common good.

Some who study human motivation assert that the money people earn as wages is not the prime motivating factor in their lives. They want to feel they are contributing in a positive way to their society. They want a sense of accomplishment that goes beyond their jobs. The designated portion of the company contribution does just that. It links people's work to the common good.

They may vote to designate the funds to a child who needs an operation in order to stay alive. His or her picture would be enlarged into a poster hung in the workplace so even on a bad day, employees would not forget their higher purpose. Or they may want to help fund a shelter for the poor or homeless. Whatever they choose, this will add meaning to their work. This is how E2M fosters spirituality and imparts a soul to the corporation, which is normally only obligated by law to operate with the goal of producing a profit.

What's the benefit of becoming an E2M-affiliated company?

Some entrepreneurs want to share income with employees and the community, or more generously, donate stock or equity to the employees and community because they feel it is the right thing to do. Others want to become part of something with a higher purpose. They do not want to perpetuate what's happening now, or take their chances with what many feel is a doomed system. Others would feel more fulfilled joining with other members of the E2M regional shared economy to chart a new course to the shared economy and new economic era because they have a higher vision for themselves, their companies, and the community.

These are some of the socially and spiritually based reasons to join:

It makes good business sense. If a business can increase sales and profits by making a donation to the community that provides a very loyal customer base, it becomes a win-win situation for the business as well as for community members.

Very low E2M interest loans and equity funds. As the E2M Regional Economic Councils begin to establish significant amounts of community wealth, they will lend funds to E2M-affiliated businesses at loan rates as low as 1%. Thus an E2M-affiliated business can compete very strongly against businesses that are borrowing at 6%, 8%, 10 %, and even much more.

You can get friendly venture capital as a start-up company. As a venture investor, the E2M Regional Economic Council works under by-laws that discourage selling the company and its employees out to the highest bidder who will then lay off those employees and move out of town. That's a real attraction to entrepreneurs or inventors of new technologies who want to create a long-term benefit for themselves and their communities.

You have a dynamic, highly committed efficient workforce. We live in times in which there is much less mutual commitment between companies and their workforces. People change jobs more often now than in the past. Examples of corporate insensitivity are not hard to find. Stories of long-time workers receiving pink slips on a moment's notice run rampant. Often a corporation will purchase a profitable business selling similar products, then sell any off duplicate assets, close the business's facilities, lay off long-time workers, and service the company's customers from another office. This is a very effective way to show an increase in profits. It serves the company and its investors well, but the employees are the losers. E2M-certified companies, owned by the community, are not held to the same demands by investors. The community would be happy to be an owner of a successful business employing local people in long-term jobs, producing a good product while earning adequate profits. People holding jobs in such a company are much more likely to feel secure, much less likely to quit their jobs, and much more a part of the company.

I could cite many more examples of companies not caring about employees, but there is another side of this to consider that relates to employees. There is a growing angst by employees towards their companies, too. Polls show that far too many employees are unhappy in typical corporate environments and are not engaged in their jobs.[26] We've all heard people "bad-rapping" their bosses and companies; and it is often quite justified.

However, if E2M-affiliated companies are willing to make commitments to their communities and employees that go beyond the corporate call of duty, employees also need to return that respect, and it has been shown that they will.[27] In most cases there needs to be an educational process, because companies with employees who are engaged and care about each other and the company will be more successful. E2M cannot achieve its full potential if employees come in to work with bad attitudes. There is no room for lack of dedication between management and employees in an E2M-certified company. In an E2M-certified company there is a different vision for its employees. We expect its managers and employees to have a different vision for their company.

History shows that when you actively care about and share with your employees, they begin to care about their companies. An example I'll give you is Stanhome Products. My friend, the former CFO of Stanhome, was telling me that when he was a young man and newly employed manager, he was making his first visit to the Stanhome manufacturing facility in Easthampton, Mass. When he walked into the production area, he was pleasantly surprised when employees, with smiles on their faces, invited him to come over to their work stations so they could show him what they were doing. They were excited about their jobs and about the chance to educate this new young manager about the manufacturing processes. At that time, there were 1,200 folks working there. The average term of service of those folks was 22 years! That

---

[26] http://www.gallup.com/poll/181289/majority-employees-not-engaged-despite-gains-2014.aspx
[27] Google, Inc would be an excellent example.

was the average. That meant a good number of employees had worked there for 40 or 50 years. Mothers and fathers were passing jobs down to their children. There was a waiting list of thousands of people who wanted to work for Stanhome. That's what a company and workforce with commitment to each other looks like.

When you treat your employees well, they will reward you for it. If you have a highly efficient committed workforce, you eliminate unproductive time, worker turnover, and even sick time out. Some estimates say that a large part of a business's cost is unproductive time, turnover and associated retraining expenses, and other indirect costs. These are some of the advantages that E2M affiliation can bring to a business.

For those E2M-certified Gold Level companies that choose to donate stock to the community, that donated stock would be non-voting stock. The community is not going to come in and tell you how to run your business. Entrepreneurs and their employees know best how to run their companies. They do not need a committee of people telling them how things should be run. We need to keep these businesses powerful, competitive and highly focused on succeeding without interference from the community. Thus donated stock carries no vote.

Most important, E2M-affiliated businesses and products will be sought out by community members who want to support a company choosing to do good. Such companies not only serve the community's interests, they serve their own. This is another important component of the E2M model; it links our own self-interests to that of the community. The more we seek to increase our own personal and financial conditions as entrepreneurs, the more we bring the community along. Some people have told me it helps them to ease the "guilt" they have about wanting to make significant amounts of money. I will say I applaud anyone wanting to become wealthy, so long as they contribute to the health of the community that blesses them with wealth. For those who feel they are already doing this by paying taxes, I would submit that those in control of tax-based funds are not going to deliver us the shared economy we desire, or we would already have it.

The Community

So now we have a means to gather wealth from the economic system using E2M-certified and affiliated businesses, and we have a means to hold and control that wealth through the E2M Regional Economic Councils. But where is this wealth coming from? That is the third component of E2M. It is the source of wealth, and it is the community itself, the millions of people who make purchases every day.

Most of the wealth controlled by the very people who stand in the way of economic change receive that wealth from the community through the more than $10 trillion it spends each year for goods and services produced by investor-owned companies. By redirecting these purchases to E2M businesses as community-owned or community-shared companies, the community can be a very powerful force to create community wealth for itself rather than for those who would deny the change we need to create a sustainable and community-controlled society.

So just as a laser aligns normally weak rays of light into beams powerful enough to vaporize metal, E2M enables communities to direct normally uncoordinated economic transactions into streams of money powerful enough to change the world.

By creating these streams of money, consumers can make any number of companies very successful. When E2M-certified or affiliated businesses are successful, they generate income for the E2M Regional Economic Councils. And when the E2M Regional Economic Councils have income, they can begin to transform the community.

U.S. consumers spend more than $10 trillion on goods and services every year. That could assure success to five million companies selling $2 million a year of products and services. That would be more than the total number of businesses employing from one to 99 people each in 2004![28] The community can make any business it wants successful because ultimately it is the community that decides whether a business succeeds. So E2M.org will help educate and encourage community members to seek out E2M businesses and products. If you see the E2M tri-spiral logo on a business's literature or products, buy from them because you are invested in and benefit from that business.

This does not require any special effort on the part of the members of the general public who choose to support the E2M regional shared economy, the E2M Regional Economic Council, and E2M-affiliated businesses. In fact, the goal of E2M is to achieve maximum impact with minimum effort. E2M does not ask community members to donate their money or their time to create enormous change. People are already too stretched for time and money. True change in these overwhelming and burdensome times comes most easily when it requires minimal time, money, or effort on the part of the populace. That is why we only ask the general public to take simple actions that they are already doing and just do it in a slightly different way.

---

[28] In 2004 the US Census reported that there were 4,980,165 firms employing from 1 to 99 employees. These represented 84% of all businesses with employees and 36.4% of all US employees. http://www.census.gov/epcd/www/smallbus.html

Because making purchases is one of our most common and simple daily activities, we can simply purchase products of equal or better quality at the same or lower prices from E2M-affiliated businesses. The more purchases community members make from E2M-affiliated businesses, the more money the community earns.

Through taking these simple actions by looking for the E2M tri-spiral logo, or seeking out companies or products at our websites at www.e2m.org or www.communityage.org, community members can achieve massive transformative change with minimal amount of activity. People must shop regularly and they only need to keep an eye open for the tri-spiral logo on E2M-supportive products to begin to change their world.

It has already been shown that community members will support businesses that "do good." In our initial tests, we sold E2M Community Coffee from just one 12" x 16" display at the Big E market in Easthampton, Mass. Our coffee was of a better quality than a good number of our competitors and our prices were lower! We sold thousands of dollars of coffee from that location alone with no advertising. As we expanded to several outlets, sales over several years exceeded $50,000.

On a larger scale, Newman's Own, a business started by the late actor Paul Newman, is a wonderful example. Newman started the business with the intent of donating its profits to great causes such as Hole in the Wall camps, which provide recreation to many needy or ill children. He began selling $2 to $3 dollar bottles of salad dressing and did so well that the company now sells coffee, cookies, popcorn, and many other products. As a result, since the company started making donations in 1982, Newman's Own has donated more than $250 million to charities!

That's just what one company can do. Image what we could do with 1,000,000 members of the public committed to supporting E2M companies and products! At an average income of $40,000 per year, if these one million people spent only ten percent of their income with E2M companies, that would equal $4 billion of sales, which could support 2,000 small businesses doing $2 million a year each in business and could create from $20 million to $80 million or more in community wealth. If that 1,000,000 people became 70,000,000, the community wealth created could range from $1.4 billion to $14 billion.[29] Seventy million people is a fair approximation of the number of women in the consumer sector in the U.S. It is the number of union members we once had in the U.S. It is also the number of evangelicals who have a common purpose. These figures show how many people can get together under a common banner if they believe the cause is just.

One of the goals of E2M is to help educate people to the fact that they should support these businesses and products to help make them successful. When other entrepreneurs see E2M-affiliated businesses become successful, they're going to want to join in. It will soon become obvious that the way to make a sustainable business is to produce a good product that the community needs and share its wealth with the community that could beat a path to its door or website to purchase products or services.

That is what makes this relationship between the community and the businesses so powerful. By proactively purchasing E2M-labeled products from E2M-certified or affiliated companies that are dedicated to a common purpose, we create

---

[29] This assumes these businesses donated from one half to two percent of their gross income to E2M Economic Communities. The above amounts do not include the market value of any company equity owned by the community and could increase the amount of community wealth considerably.

immense flows of monies to be used to transform our world and to begin the establishment of the shared economy.

This simple quid-pro-quo purchasing strategy also is what enables the members of the community to create the maximum impact on their community while minimizing the effort required to do so.

Another very important characteristic of E2M is that it allows a people who are already overtaxed, overworked, and overwhelmed to become less paralyzed by those burdens and to stand up for themselves in a very powerful way. This way makes the transformative socioeconomic changes necessary to open the door to the next economic era.

As we create more E2M products made and distributed by E2M-affiliated companies and actively supported by millions of consumers, we will surely become one of the most powerful economic forces in the country, if not the world. With that economic power, we can usher in a new community-controlled economy for the good of all. How fast it happens is completely under our control.

Happiness comes when your work and words are of benefit to yourself and others.

~Buddha

Individual commitment to a group effort – that is what makes a team work, a company work, a society work, a civilization work.

~Vince Lombardi, Coach

Chapter 14 - A Summary of the Shared Economy

I began writing this book in November 2009, 10 years after I first received the E2M idea. Much has been done in that time to develop the first E2M regional shared economy here in Western Massachusetts. We have garnered the support of federal and local elected officials, educators, economists, entrepreneurs, labor leaders, students, and community members. We formed E2M.org, a federally recognized nonprofit organization, to expand the model. We established the E2M Regional Economic Council of Western Massachusetts to serve this first pilot region, and created all the legal, financial, and organizational documents and contracts necessary to expand the E2M model in our mission to be a catalyst for the shared economy. However, we have just begun; this book is our first effort to tell our story on a broader stage so other regions around the country and world can consider joining us.

As more regions develop E2M regional shared economies and the E2M movement expands, these decentralized yet economically connected communities will act independently to serve the common good in their regions. They could also act collectively using their combined economic power to address national or global issues. As these regional communities grow more community wealth, they will develop the same extraordinary level of economic power now enjoyed by only very wealthy individuals and large corporations. When administered by nonprofit E2M Regional Councils not owned by any individual and not driven by greed, communities can use this newfound power to serve the good of all in a new vision for a new society. Thus we will witness the birth of a compassionate, caring, sharing economic network unfettered by geographical borders, in which communities become more powerful than corporations and people become more valued than profits.

From a broader perspective, E2M creates a mutually beneficial link between the commercial and social sectors of our society. As long as money flows within the commercial sectors of an E2M regional shared economy, it will always flow to the social sector through the E2M infrastructure. As the E2M Regional Economic Councils acquire this money, they will spend it on community and economic development initiatives, thus returning that money right back into the community; then the process begins all over again. Because their income is generated by consumer sales, E2M Regional Economic Councils know they will always have money coming in. Thus they will always be putting it right back into the community. This is a circular cash flow in which money is always in motion. In order to do the most good and impart its energy, money must be moving. E2M keeps money moving and doing good rather than what is now happening in the current economy in which money accumulates in the hands of the few, creating economic stagnation.

Because of this circular cash flow, the concept of "losing money" in an E2M regional shared economy is quite different than in the current economy in which losing money means that a person or institution that had the money no longer has it for whatever reason. Consider this example in an E2M regional shared economy. The local E2M Regional Economic Council lends money to a small restaurant that loses the money and that E2M Regional Economic Council is not repaid. How did the restaurant lose the money? It spent it on food, paper goods, wages, rents, and other items. Although the restaurant did not make that money back, it still put it out into the community where it created a benefit to other small businesses and employees. In other words, it did produce some positive result for someone. If the E2M Regional Economic Council's purpose is to do good, then that restaurant succeeded although on a secondary level rather than directly with the original borrower. Because the E2M Regional Economic Council receives income from economic transactions, the money it lost is eventually going to come right back to the Council, thus it did good and the Council still eventually gets the money back.

So, as money continuously flows in this circular cash flow for the common good, it will pass through the hands of the many and will impart great energy that can transform lives, create new opportunities, clean the environment, create greater hope, and ensure the continuation of a healthy social sector. This is good not only for the social sector, but also for the commercial sector, which cannot survive without a healthy social sector. Everybody wins.

At this time in the journey of humanity, we are now approaching either the edge of a cliff or the threshold of a new future. The choice is ours. The age of industrial capitalism, which enriches the few at the expense of the many, has been successful in creating many new technologies ranging from the cotton gin to the computer. Our technological breakthroughs have given us the ability to connect globally and have made the world a smaller place. However, because much of the industrial/technology era was based on maximizing profits and growth, it has taken us to the current unsustainable reality.

We must appreciate that era for the good that it has done, but a change is needed to ensure that all of us are blessed with the wonders that our planet offers. That the current economic system is not sustainable is now accepted by millions of people who are watching our system flounder, our social fabric unweave, and our environment decline. It is time for a change. That time is now. It is our time and it is our choice.

It is also easy to start. All you need to do is find seven other people in your region who want to change the world for a better place. Get yourselves together, contact E2M.org, and you will have taken a huge step in the right direction.

Every one of you who is reading this book has the opportunity to create great change. You may be a worker, a homemaker, an entrepreneur, a spiritual leader, the president of a large organization, or even the president of a nation. E2M provides you an opportunity to create change, even great change. If we choose change, we can enter the next economic era. No one can deny us.

It is ours for the taking.

I look forward confidently to the day when all who work for a living will be one. This will be the day when we bring into full realization the American dream – a dream yet unfulfilled. A dream of equality of opportunity, of privilege and property widely distributed; a dream of a land where men will not take necessities from the many to give luxuries to the few; a dream of a land where men will not argue that the color of a man's skin determines the content of his character; a dream of a nation where all our gifts and resources are held not for ourselves alone, but as instruments of service for the rest of humanity; the dream of a country where every man will respect the dignity and worth of the human personality.

~Martin Luther King, Jr.

Never doubt that a small, group of thoughtful, committed citizens can change the world. Indeed, it is the only thing that ever has.

~Margaret Mead, anthropologist

Chapter 15 - Fast Track to the Shared Economy

The establishment of a shared economy would have a significant positive impact on many institutions and peoples. Some groups that have much to gain from the rise of the shared economy currently possess such enormous potential power that they alone could be great catalysts to open the doors to the shared economy virtually immediately. Let's take a closer look at a few to see how they might benefit and help create the new age. I've chosen those that I feel are the most important. They are students and the young, women, faith-based organizations, unions, universities, farmers, governments, emerging countries, and the wealthy.

I am including a discussion about the wealthy as well. While some feel they are part of the problem and may resist a shared economy, I cannot accept that position. The rich have the most to lose from the failure of the current economic system. Thus, although they may not be catalysts for a great movement into the next era, their situation certainly merits discussion.

Understanding the role major religions have on the world stage, I felt it would also be important to spend some time considering how people of faith and leaders of the faithful might look upon the E2M Economic Model as the foundational economic system that could give rise to the shared economy. The current economic system based on a "survival of the fittest" and "get as much as you can, while you can" mentality is not in harmony with the most basic principles of any major religion. I believe a case can be made showing that the E2M Economic Model is in alignment both spiritually and pragmatically with the principles set forth in the major faith-based organizations. If so, using the E2M model to create a shared economy provides millions of the faithful and their leaders with an unprecedented opportunity to embark on refreshing new directions that such a synergy between religion and economics could offer.

As you know, I am a common man and do not consider myself a scholar on religious matters, but based on some events, personal meetings, and research I have done, I will present my views on this subject to the best of my ability.

When one door of happiness closes, another opens; but often we look so long at the closed door that we do not see the one which has been opened for us.

~Helen Keller

Civilization can only revive when there shall come into being in a number of individuals a new tone of mind, independent of the prevalent one among the crowds, and in opposition to it – a tone of mind which will gradually win influence over the collective one, and in the end determine its character. Only an ethical movement can rescue us from barbarism, and the ethical comes into existence only in individuals.

~Albert Schweitzer

When we are in partnership and have stopped clutching each other's throats, when we have stopped enslaving each other, we will stand together, hands clasped, and be friends. we will be comrades, we will be brothers, and we will begin the march to the grandest civilization the human race has ever known.

~Eugene V. Debs, Indiana State Senator, 1880

Chapter 16 - Students and the Young

I believe this millennial generation is the most important generation in the history of humanity. Today's students and the young will be the generation that determines who will control our planet – communities serving the common good, or large multinational corporations and banks bent on maximizing profits and growth for a relatively few investors. In fact, I believe this is the calling of the millennial generation. If communities control the planet, we will have a chance at a sustainable planet. If corporations and bankers control the planet, we will experience more of the same situation that threatens our freedoms, financial security, and environmental and personal health.

At no time in history has it been more important for the young to stand up for themselves and use the power they possess to guide society in a new direction. The young do not have to accept what is being handed to them in the way of an unsustainable, unethical, and even immoral economic system that stacks the deck against their generation. The young can say "Thanks, but no thanks. We have a different view of a future for ourselves and we are going to make it so. We refuse any longer to be fodder for the corporate and financial interests that plan to maximize benefits for themselves by further indebting us, disempowering us, or dismissing us. We are going to stand up to this economic heresy against humankind and create the change necessary for the betterment of our country, our democracy, our parents, our brothers and sisters, and ourselves." This is within the purpose of today's youth, and it is critical that they see the truth.

Many of history's great movements began with students. I remember my own youth in the 1960's when the issues of the day were the civil rights and peace movements. In those days, there was a saying that became popular: "Don't trust anyone over 30." There was a generation gap that was insurmountable. I remember thinking, "I can't wait to get older so my generation can develop the power to do what is right." Well, that thinking was faulty in that there were many people over 30 that were sympathetic to the concerns of the young; on the other hand, many of those young went on to become co-opted by the very system they railed against in their youth. The emergence of yuppies was a good example of how many of the young became co-opted.

The lesson here is that there is nothing to be gained by waiting for the future. The young must use their power now. It is also folly for the young to expect those in seats of great power to sacrifice their own comforts to help the young create the world they want and need. Yes, the young will surely be able to find some in power who truly care for them, but before they find those elders, they must first find themselves.

The young do not have an unlimited amount of time to learn that change does not come about from the efforts of those who have acquired power. Powerful people are not going to compromise themselves or their wealth by advocating for the young or for any type of significant change. Neither does change come from the efforts of those who are complacent, fearful, or paralyzed by the status quo. Change only comes from tension caused by the pressure of knowing that the status quo is not acceptable.

An excerpt from a book written in the 1960s comes to mind:

"Most of what is happening that is new, provocative and engaging in politics, education, the arts, and social relations is the creation of either youth, who are profoundly, even fanatically, alienated from the parental generation, or those who address themselves primarily to the young."

"If the resistance of the counterculture fails, I think there will be nothing in store for us but what anti-utopians like Huxley and Orwell have forecast…"

"But if one believes, as I do, that the alienated young are giving shape to something that looks like the saving vision our endangered civilization requires, then there is no avoiding the need to understand them and educate them in what they are about."

"The Making of a Counter Culture"
by Theodore Roszak, (Doubleday, 1969)

The young are particularly powerful for another reason. You have seen how the E2M model places power in the hands of communities by coordinating normally uncoordinated purchases. Because the generation ranging in age from 15 to 34 is the most powerful consumer sector in our society, that sector can create the most impact in moving into the new economic era.

As a catalyst to advance the onset of an alternative economy, the young are a very powerful group that, in themselves, can open the door to that shared economy. They do not need anyone else except themselves. If they can overcome the normal skepticism felt when someone says you are more powerful than you think, then change can come.

To this end, I am writing this book with the students and the young in mind. In the early development of the E2M model, young people inspired some important adjustments that were made to the original vision. It was students who drove those changes. In 2001, American International College students were very excited about E2M, but at that time the only corporate model I specified gave control of the businesses to the community allied with either the entrepreneur or investor. Young entrepreneurs wanted to control their own businesses, thus the model was expanded to include businesses who donated equity, but not by ceding control. That opened even more possibilities for existing businesses.

The second group of students to help define the E2M model was the Student Government Association (SGA) we worked with in 2003 at the University of Massachusetts at Amherst. Those students felt that the members of the E2M Regional Economic Councils should be democratically elected to those seats through a popular election. The E2M board could not comply due to the fact that popular elections can be controlled more easily by those with wealth, as is often seen in political elections in which the candidate with the most money to spend wins.

However, the board did recognize that, as students suggested, an element of democracy needed to be incorporated into the E2M Regional Economic Councils to preserve their integrity. Thus it was decided that although new members of the board would be elected by the existing members, there would be a democratic process that could be used to remove any member of the E2M Regional Economic Council who proved to be unworthy of the position.

The UMass Student Government Association's input was critical, and that group went on to sponsor and pass legislation within the SGA, representing 18,000 students, calling for the University to study ways to incorporate E2M into the University community. The E2M board and I were very appreciative of the input of American International College and UMass-Amherst students who proved that the young are much more creative and open to change than those in power at those same institutions.

I remember my student days clearly and am committed to enabling the young to use the power they already possess to open the doors to the shared economy before it is too late.

E2M has now sparked the interest of students at Hampshire College, an institution known for its unique approach to education, high caliber of thinking, and the freedom to explore new paradigms. At Hampshire College, students are free from pressure to comply with the status quo or to become cogs in the wheels of an increasingly inhuman corporate machine bent on maximizing efficiencies, profits, and growth. Hampshire College itself, unlike research institutions relying on corporate donations, is less likely to be influenced by those corporations and venture capitalists that are now becoming more powerful factors in determining the educational curriculum of public research institutions.

If students at these schools connect with their peers at other nearby colleges, they can align themselves as a consumer base and economic force that can recruit many small local businesses into the E2M regional shared economy and patronize them whenever possible. As a group, the young can also create movements that think local and act globally as student organizations become committed to the shared economy. Such organizations might include student-led activist, political and religious organizations, as well as entrepreneurial groups emerging within the schools of business.

I am very hopeful that the students and youth of the world will show themselves to be the sleeping giant that awakens to take on the serious challenges imposed upon them by those who promote and maintain the status quo. I am hopeful that they will rise up to recognize and use the power they possess to become a major catalyst for world change and entry into the shared economy.

On April 20, 2010 Archbishop Desmond TuTu addressed an audience of students at American International College in Springfield, Mass. and left them this message:

> I salute you and say, 'Please remain idealistic.' Many young people believe it is possible for there to be a world without war. They believe it is possible to have a world without poverty.
>
> I say to you, 'Don't be infected by the cynicism of oldies like us.'
>
> Dream of a different kind of world, a world in which all God's children are sisters and brothers, have enough to eat, have enough clean water to drink, have a good education, and good health care. It's possible!"

I couldn't agree more, and I hope students everywhere will understand the importance of the Archbishop's comment. The "look and feel" of the future will be determined by what the young choose to do.

The status quo is no longer acceptable; change is crucial; and the young must rise to the occasion. When they do, I think they will be pleasantly surprised to find out that their elders will willingly and happily follow.

Education either functions as an instrument which is used to facilitate integration of the younger generation into the logic of the present system and bring about conformity or it becomes the practice of freedom, the means by which men and women deal critically and creatively with reality and discover how to participate in the transformation of their world

~Paulo Freire

The future belongs to those who give the next generation reason for hope.

~Pierre Teilhard de Chardin, French Jesuit philosopher

The revolution has always been in the hands of the young. The young always inherit the revolution.

~Huey Newton, Co-founder Black Panther Party

The young do not know enough to be prudent, and therefore they attempt the impossible -- and achieve it, generation after generation.

~Pearl S. Buck, Write,/Nobel Laureate

The master's tools will never dismantle the master's house. They may allow us temporarily to beat him at his own game, but they will never allow us to bring about genuine change.

~Audre Lorde, Caribbean-American
writer, poet and activist

Status quo, you know, that is Latin for "'the mess we're in."

.   ~Ronald Reagan

Chapter 17 - Women

As a man with a history of commercial entrepreneurship, I can't help but see myself as a warrior in the field of commerce. There is much in the male-dominated commercial sector that is repugnant to me as a human being. Such clichés as "Good guys finish last" or "Sorry, nothing personal, it's just business" speak to the current situation quite effectively.

For the most part, one must always be on the defensive in the dog-eat-dog world of commerce. Although my business in other countries was easier, I was always focused on the fact that in the USA, someone was usually trying to eat my or my employee's lunch every day. I was always prepared to be someone's good friend or formidable adversary depending on their manner of doing business or their treatment of me. Even when I took a break from my commercial entrepreneurial career to become a social entrepreneur, this instinct to watch my back did not completely subside. In fact, in the early days of E2M when I had just left my manufacturing business, I was talking to another social entrepreneur and expressed my happiness about leaving the dog-eat-dog commercial world for the nonprofit world of service. This person laughed and said, "Boy are you in for a surprise. It's worse in the nonprofit world where everyone is scrambling for a very limited amount of grant money, donations, or other funding."

I found this person's warning to be true when I saw how little collaboration exists among nonprofits, and in fact how he himself had not been successful of ridding himself of self-serving tendencies. A new way of doing business is required if we are to evolve to a higher place, and I am afraid that our male-dominated, testosterone-driven commercial sector is more limited in its ability to intellectually embrace that which we need, to take our society into a new era.

Women, on the other hand, offer more hope. That being said, I know some women who can match any man in purely ruthless, competitive, and self-serving attributes that point up the worst of human possibilities. However, for the most part, I have greater hope and faith in the larger population of self-confident, empathetic, and nurturing women as a wonderful force to bring us all together.

The current economic system is all about competition, winning, hunting, battle, and survival of the fittest. E2M and the shared economy are about nurturing, caring, sharing, loving each other, and working for the benefit of all. It is maternal in nature. It is what this planet needs. A warm-hearted, nurturing, service-oriented, and loving element that is necessary for long-term survival of the species. It is my hope that women, as the primary caretakers and consumers, will embrace the shared economy at this time when the status quo has failed billions of us.

We know that women have faced gender-based obstacles as more of them entered the male-dominated commercial sector. As a result, their power to create change has been stifled. However, as a force capable of creating the great change that would come with a shared economy, women's power could be unparalleled. This does not require a "women's movement" per se, for movements that focus on one group over another are not necessary when one has the power to create change at will. As the predominant consumer force as well, women already have that power! Now all that is required is to draw on their intellect and nurturing instincts to do it. Women of the world, join in! The shared economy is yours if you want it.

Here's all you have to know about men and women: women are crazy, men are stupid. And the main reason women are crazy is that men are stupid.

~George Carlin, comedian

Whatever women do they must do twice as well as men to be thought half as good. Luckily, this is not difficult.

~Charlotte Whitton, Canadian feminist
and Ottawa mayor

If you want anything said, ask a man. If you want something done, ask a woman.

~Margaret Thatcher

The earth is ready, the time is ripe, for the authoritative expression of the feminine...

~Anna Garlin Spencer, educator,
Unitarian minister

Chapter 18 – Faith-Based Organizations

There exists one group of billions of souls who subscribe to ideals they feel, if attained, would be of great benefit to humanity. Millions of these people passionately pursue these ideals every day by taking action in areas they feel can lead to a greater future. Who are these millions? They are those who have committed themselves to live by the values of the great religious leaders whom they worship every day. They are the ones who have accepted a God, Jesus Christ, Allah, Muhammad, Buddha, or other spiritual leaders into their lives. They are the faithful.

If one is to propose that a new economic era is possible by using an alternative economic model to create a shared economy for the common good, there needs to be an understanding of how compatible that proposed shared economy would be with the ideals of the faithful as expressed by the predominant religions of the world.

As someone who is more spiritual than religious, I try to embrace the best aspects of a number of religions while maintaining my own beliefs and ethics. Thus, my perception of the compatibility of E2M with faith-based organizations or with religious doctrine comes more from what others have told me, while complemented by some of my own research and beliefs.

I will share some of my feelings and experiences as it relates to religious doctrines. As imperfect as my religious knowledge may be, I will do my best, and will rely on you to fill in the blanks or to build on the seeds sown in the religious doctrines listed below in order of the number of global adherents.

Christianity

Christians believe in the existence of one God. They accept Jesus Christ as the Son of God, the savior of humanity, and the Messiah as prophesied in the Old Testament of the Holy Bible, which Christians accept as the true Word of God. Christians believe that Jesus was born to the Virgin Mary, lived among us as a teacher and prophet, then suffered and died by crucifixion for our sins. He was resurrected then ascended to Heaven to open the doors to those who accept Him as their Savior. Christians believe that Jesus Christ, as the physical incarnation of God, was the model of a virtuous life. Some of the virtues considered important by Christians are benevolence, charity, citizenship, equity, forgiveness, generosity, helpfulness, honor, independence, individualism, industriousness, nurturing, optimism, responsibility, self-confidence, sharing, spirituality, and thankfulness.

Hundreds of millions of Christians have accepted an ethic based on these and other virtues including caring for their fellow men and women, loving each other, and doing unto others as we would have them do unto us.

Unfortunately, an economic system that includes or even upholds elements of greed, unrestrained competition, survival of the fittest, exploitation of the many by the few, economic subjugation of the masses, expansion of poverty and hunger, and other maladies does not sit well within Christian principles.

Thus millions of Christians go to church each week then walk out of the parish halls into a world driven by what many believe to be an immoral and unethical economic system that has little compatibility with their more humane and spiritual desires and needs. Many are warmhearted, loving people who leave home every day after hugging and kissing their spouses and children, then go into large national or multinational corporate environments to do the deeds expected of them by an invisible, over-lording group of investors interested in one thing – money, and as much of it as they can get their hands on. It has been said that 50% to 70% of people hate their jobs! Part of it has certainly to do with the dichotomy between their personal and spiritual beliefs and the persona they adopt in their soul-less, unloving corporate environments.

For these people, the advent of the shared economy with its E2M Regional Economic Councils based on caring, sharing, and loving, rather than on greed and exploitation, could provide a way for them to remain connected to their humanity while operating in the real world. E2M enables Christians to maintain their Christian ethics because E2M was created based on those same Christian ethics. Although I have felt this since the time I received E2M, it was brought home to me in a powerful way while watching the recent Michael Moore movie titled "Capitalism– A Love Story." Moore was interviewing Father Dick Preston, who felt that capitalism, as currently practiced, is contrary to all that is good, contrary to all major religions, and precisely what holy books say is unjust. Supportive of Father Preston's comments was Father Peter Dougherty who, as a Catholic priest for 45 years, felt this economic system was immoral and radically evil. He was taken aback by systemic propaganda that results in the ability to convince the people who are victimized by it to support it. Further, Bishop Thomas Gumbleton of the Archdiocese of Detroit said the "system doesn't seem to be providing for the well-being of all the people."

These are all profound statements with which I can easily concur. Even more important to me, these views have profound consequences for E2M as an alternative, ethical, economic system. By recognizing E2M as an alternative economic system, Christians now have a choice of which economic system to use, the one that is a sin or the one that is not. Thus, they would no longer be forced by a lack of options to embrace a system which is a sin in the eyes of the Bishop of Chicago, in the eyes of the Church, or in the eyes of God.

A friend of mine who is a pastor in an inner-city African-American church said this in a different way. He told me that many Christians, particularly evangelicals, have begun to target their efforts to make improvements in two contemporary areas – the deterioration of the environment and the massive expansion of personal and household debt. In environmental issues, conservative Christians and evangelicals have collaborated with liberals in the environmental movement. This surprising coalition is based on the fundamental evangelical belief that the environment is a gift to mankind from God and it is their ecumenical duty to help prevent the desecration of God's gift.

Secondar, the imposition of indebtedness on the masses by the financial machinations of the few is immoral in the eyes of Jesus Christ himself. This was evident by the only act of violence on the part of Jesus. He overturned the tables of the money changers in the Temple. As disgusted as Jesus was then, the same is happening today. The money changers and the Temple are different but the fact is that today the money changers (banks, credit card companies, investment houses, and the people who lead them) have surely infected the Temple of Life. Millions, if not billions, of people are subjected to the negative effects of the financial and life-
challenging schemes of those who have insatiable appetites for ever-increasing profits and growth and who cannot accept that enough is enough. Today's money changers seem to be not too dissimilar from those of Jesus' time.

The pastor at the Mount Carmel Baptist Church in Norfolk, Va. is another example of someone who feels debt is onerous. In his parish, the members create a fund and select one parishioner at random to receive those funds to pay off all personal debt except for the home mortgage and car loan. Thus, given a clean slate, that parishioner can start life over without the grips of the beast of debt.

Given such a clean slate, one must understand that although the masses are encouraged to take on debt by advertisers, banks, investment houses, and other institutions, it is still one's personal choice to actually agree to the debt. We must all reevaluate our relationship with money, our susceptibility to messages that advocate debt, and learn to live more simply. It is a well-known economic fact that once people's income meets their basic needs, the continual acquisition of material things does not bring a higher level of happiness. However, the money changers would encourage us to continue along our wayward paths because it is in their best interests.

It is time to eliminate the effect of the modern-day money changers on the modern-day lives of millions, and E2M can do just that, my pastor friend tells me. In expressing his support of E2M, he said he feels confident that Jesus would approve of a system that is based on caring and sharing rather than on greed.

There are in the USA well over 100 million evangelical, African-American, Hispanic, and other Christians who believe enough is enough. Many of them understand that the economic system of the few should not be allowed to stand in the way of the transition to a new shared economy that embraces the doctrines taught by Christian leaders, including Jesus Christ himself.

I believe that any number of Christian leaders with congregations ranging in size from 10,000 to 100,000 could be catalysts to open the door to the shared economy. Just 10,000 parishioners dedicated to building an E2M regional shared economy in their region could create millions of dollars in community wealth. It is time to follow the example of Jesus Christ. It is time to, once again, overturn the tables of the money changers who have infected the Temple of Life and who are denying us a shared economy and the wonderful new economic era that it could bring.

Islam

Long before I first wrote about E2M, I read that whoever finds a way to create a positive relationship between capitalism and Islam would be doing the world a great favor. As a free market model that has been referred to as community-conscious capitalism, community capitalism, the common-good economy, and a shared economy, I was very interested in how Islam might view E2M, so I began to read about Islam. I soon realized that capitalism, as it is currently used, is not in alignment with the principles of the Quran or Islam.

Islam is based on five pillars. The first is Shahada, the belief in the oneness of the Islamic God Allah and the acceptance of Muhammad as his prophet. Salāt, as the second pillar, calls for thankful and worshipful prayer to Allah five times a day while facing Mecca, the holiest site in Islam. The third pillar, Zakāt, or alms-giving, is the practice of charitable giving by Muslims based on accumulated wealth. It is obligatory for all who are able to do so. It is considered to be a personal responsibility for Muslims to ease economic hardship for others and eliminate inequality. Zakat consists of spending 2.5% of one's wealth for the benefit of the poor or needy, including slaves, debtors and travelers.[30] Sawm, the fourth pillar, is the Islamic practice of ritual, repentant, and ascetic fasting. The fast is meant to allow Muslims to seek nearness to Allah, to express their gratitude to and dependence on him, to atone for their past sins, and to remind them of the needy.[31] As the fifth pillar, the Hajj is a pilgrimage to the holy city of Mecca to be made by every able-bodied Muslim at least once in their lifetime if he or she can afford it.

It is important to note that the pillar of Islam ranking third, after the acceptance of Allah and prayer to Allah, is Zakat, or alms-giving to care for the less fortunate.

Another important Islamic principle is the avoidance of the taking of interest in financial transactions. Al-Riba, the Muslim term for interest literally means "to excess" or "increase."

Al-Riba is considered to be "effortless profit or that profit which comes free from compensation or that extra earning obtained that is free of exchange."[32]

Al-Riba can be derived by taking interest on lent money, or taking an equal amount of superior goods in repayment for a like quantity of inferior goods. When it comes to financial transactions, Muslims "seek to avoid Riba in any of its forms, despite the fact that the basic foundation of world economics and finance today is that of riba and dealing in usury".[33]

Today's conditions were foretold by the Prophet Muhammad, who told us of a future time "when the spread of riba would be

---

[30] http://www.britannica.com/topic/Pillars-of-Islam
[31] Ibid
[32] http://www.inter-islam.org/Prohibitions/intrst.htm
[33] Ibid

so overwhelming that it would be extremely difficult for the Muslim to avoid it."[34] His warning is particularly true when we quantify the amount of interest charged in today's economic system. The U.S. government alone pays more than $380 billion of interest yearly.[35] This is more than $1,000 a year for every person in the U.S. population. When one tallies the total interest paid by all countries, states, municipalities, corporations, small businesses, and individuals, the amounts are staggering.

Thus our current economic system is incongruent with Islam, on two levels: the lack of institutionalized charity, and the proliferation of extraordinary amounts of interest payments, transaction fees, late fees, over limit fees, and other forms of "unearned" or effortless income.

This disharmony with Islam is most notable when we consider that the current economic system does not embrace, as requisite, the Islamic concept of Zakat, the third pillar. The current economic system does more to create economic inequities among people than it does to seek economic justice, as is the intention of Zakat. Charitable giving, although an option available to individuals and businesses working within the current system, is not institutionalized by that system as it is in the E2M-based shared economic system. With E2M, businesses are required to make donations as participants in the E2M regional shared economy.

Thus, in the current economic system there is great divergence from Islamic principles by the fact that much of the profit and growth of the current economic system, as well as the financial and commercial institutions that operate within it, are created by the receipt of interest paid on borrowed funds. On the

---

[34]https://muslimah2muslimah.wordpress.com/2009/12/19/avoiding-ribainterestusury/
[35] https://www.treasurydirect.gov/govt/reports/ir/ir_expense.htm

highest level in the current system, interest is paid to central banks by governments, large regional banks, and other institutions with monies created out of thin air.

Unlike the current system, in the E2M-based shared economic system, the E2M Regional Economic Councils are encouraged to charge little to no interest on loans to E2M-affiliated businesses and individuals.

Because of these two very important alignments of principles between E2M and Islam, I always believed that E2M was harmonious with the spiritual and humanitarian principles of Islam. My opportunity to find out came on November 11, 2002 when Imam W. D. Mohammed, spiritual leader of the American Muslim Society, America's largest Muslim community, visited Western Massachusetts to speak to members of the regional Muslim community.[36]

Because he was the most prominent Muslim leader in America, I was hoping to meet the Imam to discuss E2M and get an idea of how compatible with Islam it might be as a new model of capitalism. Following the Imam's speech about Ramadan, I requested, and was granted, a short meeting with him. I explained my desire to formalize E2M as an alternative economic model and outlined the salient points as I thought they related to the principles of Islam as I understood them.

After several minutes, the Imam reached out and took my arm, smiled at me, told me he thought I was doing wonderful work, then asked me for my business card. When I handed him my card, he took his pen and in a somewhat less than smooth handwriting consistent with his age, wrote something down.

---

[36] http://www.smith.edu/newsoffice/releases/02-031.html

He handed it back to me and said, "I like what you are doing; this is my home address and telephone number. When you feel your work is complete and you are ready, please call me and come for a visit."

I knew I still had years to go before my own work would be complete enough to take the Imam up on his invitation. I thanked him for his interest and left buoyed by his positivity.

My work is now complete but I am saddened that I cannot deliver it personally to Imam W.D. Mohammed as he requested. The Imam passed away on September 9, 2009. I will always remember the Imam's warm, smiling eyes as I described E2M. and I hope it is something that can be embraced by Muslims everywhere.

Hinduism

Hinduism is the predominant religion of India. It is the world's third largest religion, after Christianity and Islam, with more than a billion adherents.

Hinduism embraces a number of differing beliefs and has no single founder. Its origins can be traced back as far as the Iron Age in India, thus it is considered by many to be the oldest living religion. Hinduism does not center around one common religious doctrine, but is composed of many traditions. The major traditions in Hinduism are Vaishnavism, Shaivism, Smartism and Shaktism.

Hindus do not embrace one written holy text but rather a number of writings and beliefs originating with early Vedic writings. These texts teach adherents such matters as theology, philosophy and mythology, and provide information on the practice of religious living (dharma). Among these texts, the Vedas are the foremost in authority, importance and antiquity.

The Hindu concept of God is complex and varies among differing Hindu traditions. Many Hindus recognize numerous divine beings, which are subordinate to a Supreme Being. Hinduism embraces a belief in reincarnation (samsara) and karma, as well as in personal duty, or dharma. Karma is that outcome which one brings upon oneself, in this life or in future reincarnations, from their deeds in this lifetime, both good and bad. The effects of karma are believed to be felt in our past, present, or future experiences, for all time.

Hinduism teaches that we all experience continual cycles of death and reincarnation. By attaining positive karma, this cycle will end as we take our eternal place in union with the Supreme Being. In Hinduism, the human experience is not determined by the will of God as is the belief of Christians, Jews, and Muslims. Hindus believe we all have free will to choose between good or evil. Therefore, depending on our actions, we will achieve a positive or negative karma. It is at the will of God that we will ultimately experience the good or bad consequences of our karma.

Under Hindu doctrine, there are four objectives in human life: dharma (righteousness), artha (livelihood and wealth), kama (sensual pleasure), and moksha (liberation/freedom). One may attain these life objectives throughout several stages of life. The first part of one's life, Brahmacharya, the stage as a student, is spent in celibate, controlled, sober and pure contemplation under the guidance of a Guru, building up the mind for spiritual knowledge. Grihastha is the householder's stage, in which one marries and satisfies kama and artha in one's married and professional life, respectively. The moral obligations of a Hindu householder include supporting one's parents, children, guests and holy figures. Vanaprastha, the retirement stage, is gradual detachment from the material world. This may involve giving over duties to one's children, spending more time in religious practices and embarking on holy pilgrimages. Finally, in Sannyasa, the stage of solemnity, one renounces all worldly attachments to find, in seclusion, the Divine through detachment from worldly life and to peacefully shed the body for moksha.

Hinduism teaches that the ultimate goal of life, referred to as moksha, nirvana or samadhi, is:

- the realization of one's union with God
- the realization of one's eternal relationship with God
- the realization of the unity of all existence
- perfect unselfishness and knowledge of the Self
- the attainment of perfect mental peace
- detachment from worldly desires

Such realization liberates one from samsara, thus ending the cycle of rebirth.

E2M is compatible with Hinduism because, as an economic model, it subscribes to the goal of improving the human experience on as broad a scale as possible. E2M's purpose is to produce a healthy society by incorporating the goals of caring and sharing into the economic infrastructure, thus enhancing the possibility that each of us can meet the Hindu objectives of a thoughtful, comfortable, loving, and prosperous life. Such a life is far more likely if one frees oneself from those burdens and complexities that the current economic system places on each of us or encourages us to place upon ourselves.

I believe the possibilities for individuals and entrepreneurs to attain good karma is far greater under the E2M philosophy than under the mantra of maximizing profit and growth for the few at the expense of the many. If it is possible for corporations, having the status of personhood, to attain karma, then I believe those corporations subscribing to the tenets of the E2M model could achieve positive karma. If one were to consider societal karma, I believe that by weaving threads of caring and sharing on a wide scale into the socioeconomic fabric would increase the possibility of a society with positive karmic value.

As we create and share increasing amounts of community wealth using the E2M model, we increase the possibility for people to attain the life objectives subscribed to by Hindu traditions. The basic infrastructure of the E2M system is also complementary to the Hindu realization of unity or oneness. Under E2M, our individual transactions create wealth that E2M Regional Economic Councils share locally, nationally, and internationally. Therefore, each one of the millions of transactions taking place would have an effect elsewhere and would encourage global communications and unity.

Judaism

In my own efforts to better understand how E2M might be compatible with Judaic principles, I learned that the larger part of the Jewish population considers acceptance of Thirteen Principles of Faith to be a fundamental requirement of the Judaic religion. These embrace an acceptance and worship of one all-knowing Creator; a belief that the words of the prophets and Moses, as chief of the prophets, are true, as are the written words of the Torah, which are final and as given to Moses. Those who live by the Thirteen Principles believe there are rewards for faithfulness to them and punishment for violation of them. They further believe in the coming of a Messiah and Messianic Age.[37]

One of my business partners, a devout Jew, tells me that some believe the Messianic Age could come as a miraculous event with the arrival of the Messiah, or as an "unfoldment," by the actions of humankind, of a spiritual era favorable to the arrival of a Messiah. Many faithful Jews believe that our entry to this era is fast approaching.

For Jews, part of the observance of their Creator is to live and act in His spirit and in devotion to His ends. Under Judaic belief, the greater benefit and duty of accumulating wealth is to tithe in devotion to doing the earthly work of the Creator. This calls for charity and service to humanity.

The E2M model has a foundation based on wealth creation and charity. Unlike the current economic system based on survival of the fittest, E2M facilitates the creation of individual and community wealth to be partly used in charity and service to the common good. This requirement is in keeping with and observant of, those same requirements in Judaism. Thus, I believe E2M, as an economic infrastructure, is an enabling system that could help Jews to live within their principles in a systemic manner that is complementary to their individual beliefs and earthly actions in anticipation of a new age.

From a sociological perspective, the Jewish people have shown us that the E2M mechanism to bring people together to create community economic power has been proved historically. The Jews, as is true of the Irish, Polish, and other immigrant populations, rose in socioeconomic rank and accomplishment by dealing among themselves whenever

---

[37] http://en.wikipedia.org/wiki/Judaism

possible. By understanding the importance of collaboration among each other, these groups proved that great economic and political power can be achieved from humble, if not oppressive, beginnings.

This is the core message of E2M; if we have the faith to move forward together, acting collaboratively in using our individual economic and spiritual resources, we can all rise up and open the doors to the shared economy.

Creating Our Own Womb

As is true with people of faith, we need to gather together as people who have a hopeful vision for the future. We need to develop the faith that we can succeed in creating that future, with a refusal to be denied. We must find the common spiritual and economic threads that connect us regardless of the differences in our religious, political, or other beliefs. We must be inspired by that which connects us rather than allow our differences to disempower us. We must create a womb within, compatible with the current unsustainable economic system in which we can do business with each other, share with each other, support and care for each other, and build a great economic community dedicated to the good of all.

Just as a sick mother can give birth to a healthy child, we can plant a seed in the womb of the current unsustainable economic system to give birth to the shared economy we need to create a new economic reality and open the doors to the society we desire.

We have before us the glorious opportunity to inject a new dimension of love into the veins of our civilization...

~Reverend Martin Luther King, Jr

And the Lord said, 'Behold, the people are one, and they all have one language; and this is only the beginning of what they will do: and now nothing will be restrained from them, which they imagined to do'.

~ Genesis 11:6

Our true wealth is the good we do in this world. None of us has faith unless we desire for our neighbors what we desire for ourselves.

~Muhammad

Without faith, nothing is possible. With it, nothing is impossible.

~ Mary McLeod Bethune, African-American educator, civil rights leader, presidential advisor

Chapter 19 - Union Members and Friends

As a manufacturer for most of my life, I have seen or heard much dialogue relating to unionism. Not much of that dialogue related to me because, as a caring person, I was already treating my employees with great respect. They were accepted as members of my extended family and were paid as much as possible. Some of them made more money than I did and, as it should be, I was always the last to be paid if funds were in short supply. Thus I never administered a unionized enterprise.

Others, however, oppose the possibility of union rules that could restrict someone from doing what is necessary to ensure forward movement of the business at all times. The iconic story is of the construction site where an electrical wire is lying on a piece of lumber that needed to be moved so a forklift could gain entry to the site. The story goes that everyone had to wait for someone from the electrician's union to come to pick up the wire so someone from the carpenters union could move the lumber, so the forklift operator could move ahead. If the story is either true or possible, such restrictions can increase the costs of doing business as well as costs of manufactured products.

Often, a tension exists between the union and management, leading to negotiations in which each party attempts to get the most concessions as possible for the group they represent. This is anathema to the "enough is enough" philosophy in which each party serves and respects the other. Unfortunately, this is often characteristic of negotiators representing any group, whether it is corporate managers representing shareholders, union leaders representing workers, investment counselors representing investors, or wayward owners of some businesses who see any dollar paid to employees as a dollar not ending up in their own wallets. I was very successful in avoiding any such activities because I felt that approach did not result in a healthy enterprise.

Once I left the corporate world, I became associated with a broader spectrum of people as a community developer rather than as a commercial entrepreneur. Two of my most enjoyable relationships were with my friend Maureen Carney, a field officer for the AFL-CIO, and Jason Garand, a very nice man who is a leader at the New England Regional Council of Carpenters.

Maureen was very instrumental in pointing out that union leaders trying to organize workers to give them a voice is not all that different from employers and entrepreneurs who hire lawyers to represent their best interests in negotiations. It is more a workers rights issue then an anti-management issue. This was particularly true in the early industrial period in America in the early 1900s. My most memorable college thesis was on the plight of northern textile workers who were subjected to intolerable working conditions by self-indulgent factory owners. This issue exploded at the turn of the century as northern mills were closing down and moving to the South where wages were lower. This tension brought in the era of unionized workers, and, I might add, not without bloodshed and even murders. In one instance U.S. troops were brought in to New England as thousands of workers and supporters surged into the streets as tensions became inflamed.[38]

Many people do not realize such social upheavals ever took

---

[38] http://archives.chicagotribune.com/1934/09/11/page/1/article/three-states-call-troops-in-textile-riots

place in America, but it certainly indicated to me that any group pushed to the limit will react in the same manner. It can happen again in America if we are unable to control the continued destruction of the middle class with the result being increases in poverty, homelessness, and hopelessness.

Maureen was very helpful to me in understanding the issues as union activists see them. Jason was equally impressive as a leader for the local carpenters union. That union's expectation of its members, as employees within local businesses, exceeded even my own expectations of my employees. Jason's attitude was that if unions were going to negotiate better wages for their members than non-union employees, then those unionized workers should be expected to achieve levels of productivity that justified higher wages. He had little acceptance of union members who did not show up for work, often come in late, lean on shovels, or acted in a manner disrespectful of those employers who treated their help fairly and who were sincere in their concern for employees.

Maureen and Jason offered insight into union, employee, and workplace issues and the importance of advocacy for the worker. On a personal level, it made me even more appreciative of my own history as an employer who was very caring and appreciative of my employees. That was evidenced one day when my employees called me into the company cafeteria during a particularly stressful period for the company, and presented me with the most important sign that ever came out of Neon Technology. It was a plaque that read, "Declaration of Appreciation" and thanked me for my "contributions to science which were rivaled only by my dedication to my employees." It was a most rewarding and gratifying day for me, one that I still cherish 20 years later.

I will long remember how happy it made me to feel my caring, sharing, and love for them was recognized and appreciated, not only by a plaque, but by their everyday efforts, loyalty, and commitment. As someone who cares deeply for my employees, my interests and those of the union are essentially the same; however, some of our strategies are different.

Union leaders and management often sit on opposite sides of the negotiating table, each trying to get as much as possible for themselves or those they represent. An E2M approach could eliminate this adversarial approach while creating self-sustaining companies dedicated to the best interests of employees, unions, management, and investors.

As I pointed out earlier, of the $17 trillion in liquid investible capital in the U.S. in 2001, one percent of the population owned 50%, or $8.5 trillion. That was the bad news. The good news was that, of the remaining $8.5 trillion, union pension funds were in control of $1 trillion. As I stated in a talk I gave to a union leaders group at the Boston Social Forum in 2004, that sum is enough to create a groundswell movement towards a shared economy.

My proposal to that group was that unions invest their pension funds into E2M-certified companies, whereby the employees own a significant share. The union, as an investor, owns a substantial share, and the balance is owned by the entrepreneurs who make the business possible by providing ideas for sustainable and relevant products, technologies, or services.

By using this strategy, the union is a ready source of capital for new companies, the employees are beneficiaries of the union's goal to empower and enrich the workforce, and the entrepreneurs have outlets for their creativity and opportunities to create wealth for themselves. This arrangement also eliminates the traditional tension between unions and management due to the fact that the union is the investing partner. Anyone who has been in business knows that entrepreneurs do not create friction with their investors because they are in a partnership to make the company work. Another benefit is that unions, as investors, have the obligation to make the company work for themselves, the employees, and the entrepreneurs. Thus they will seek financial outcomes that best serve all parties. This perspective will serve all parties well, even when considering normally sticky issues such as workforce compensation and benefits. It not only requires unions to take on the role as owners when dealing with their workforces, it requires the workforces to think like the owners they are when considering how to best move the company forward.

This strategy eliminates union vs. management tensions and employee vs. management tensions, creating an environment in which all parties are dedicated to the well-being of each other as well as the community through the company's connection with the E2M Regional Economic Council.

Even more powerful is the fact that although union membership has declined over the years from more than 33% of the workforce to under 8%, there are millions of people who empathize with the plight of workers. They thus support the goals of unions that relate to the well-being of the workforce. At the height of U.S. union participation, there were 70,000,000 union members! There are still millions of supportive people including current union members, former union members, and folks who are supportive of union ideals. By actively marshalling these millions of supporters, the success of such union-launched companies can virtually be assured.

These ideas resonated with the union gathering at the 2004 Boston Social Forum. Participants included union leaders from Bar Harbor, Maine; some educators from Harvard University, members of local unions, and some local nonprofits. I was very happy to receive their interest and requests for more information, with the understanding that the E2M organization was still developing the means and methods to support interested unions.

I believe this can be the next new stage in U.S. union activity. I would like to address two points.

1. American union leaders do not want to compete with already unionized companies. I applaud this because it shows dedication to companies that are collaborating with unions, and dedication to the union members who work there. So the trades unions should not start construction competing companies, but that does not mean they can't start companies that provide supplies to construction companies, or those that produce products not related to the construction industry, such as wind turbines, alternative fuels, new technologies, food products, or other unrelated goods. With the support of millions of consumers, it is unnecessary to compete with brethren; there is a world of opportunities to implement compatible investment strategies.

2. Union leaders tell me that under scrutiny by governmental agencies, they are under the obligation to invest monies responsibly or face severe penalties. Some union financial leaders interpret this to mean that they cannot take risks but must invest money in government and blue chip securities. I beg to differ.

In the current economic system, it is in the best interests of the government and the traditional investment community to see union pension funds invested within the current financial paradigm. This perpetuates the status quo and all of the problems the current paradigm creates for millions of people. Union leaders are often not highly sophisticated financial types because many of them rose from the rank and file and are not as familiar with these matters as those who represent the interests of the investors and bankers who perpetuate the current system. Thus, some union leaders or financial managers may be easier to intimidate or coerce when it comes to financial matters.

However, it is not irresponsible to lose money on some investments. In fact, it is quite normal, as is evidenced every day in the stock market, venture capital community, and private capital community. All that is necessary to show responsibility is a clear statement of why the investor felt the investment was responsible. That argument can be supported by a well-written business plan. It can further be supported by passing business plans to a number of investors for second opinions before the union makes its own investment. By doing this, a second opinion can be established from those in the traditional financial community.

Union leaders must look back to the early 1900s when bold leaders took great risks, even with their lives, to do what they felt was right regardless of the resistance and threats of manufacturing barons who exploited workers. Today's situation is very similar to that of the past, with the exception that jobs don't go to the southern U.S. states so much as they go to China, India, Southeast Asia, Mexico – anywhere cheap labor is available.

It is true that because of union efforts, we do have weekends and vacations nowadays compared to downright oppressive environs of the early days; but much remains unchanged in that millions suffer for the benefit of the few. And many of these millions do not take weekends off or vacations anymore because they can't afford it.

Yes, it's nice to have a weekend, but what good is that if it is spent in anxiety and stress because the mortgage is unpaid, the spouse is unhappy or gone, or the kids are having problems?

Of the several already established large groups of people who can single-handedly open the doors to the shared economy, unions are a strong potential force for positive change.

It is time to hearken back to the spirit of the early union movements and its leaders to create the future we all know we want.[39]

---

[39] http://www.history.com/topics/labor

What does labor want? We want more schoolhouses and less jails; more books and less arsenals; more learning and less vice; more leisure and less greed; more justice and less revenge; in fact, more of the opportunities to cultivate our better natures, to make manhood more noble, womanhood more beautiful, and childhood more happy and bright.

~Samuel Gompers, Founder, American
Federation of Labor

Let the workers organize. Let the toilers assemble. Let their crystallized voice proclaim their injustices and demand their privileges. Let all thoughtful citizens sustain them, for the future of Labor is the future of America.

~John L. Lewis, American Labor Leader

The important role of union organizations must be admitted: their object is the representation of the various categories of workers, their lawful collaboration in the economic advance of society, and the development of the sense of their responsibility for the realization of the common good.

~Pope Paul VI

Chapter 20 - Farmers

Depending on what research you read, it is generally accepted that from 10,000 to 20,000 years ago, humans suddenly advanced from a society of hunters-gathers to a more advanced agricultural society in which humans finally learned to grow fruits and vegetables, thus becoming the first farmers. Were it not for these ancient farmers, there would be no civilization as we know it today. The emergence of this farm society was the cornerstone of the Agrarian Age. This was an age of subsistence, with people working in harmony with nature and taking care of themselves as well as their fellow community members. Agrarian values embraced the best characteristics of humankind – caring for each other, sharing the fruits of labor, working hard for the common good, connecting to the land, and establishing a sense of community.

In that age, the output of one person doing a long day's work was adequate to sustain oneself with some left over to help sustain a family member or neighbor. For such a society to work, a sense of cooperation and community were required.

However, over time, the Industrial Age emerged with the advent of machines that enabled one person to produce much more than he or she required for subsistence. Farmers were now able to sow, till, harvest, and process enough for many people, so many farmers eventually moved from the farm to the factory to operate the machines of industry. The entrepreneurial class arose, and as owners of factories, these people benefited most from the profits produced by those factories, oftentimes at the expense of employees who worked long hours at little pay and under stressful and unsafe conditions.

As wealth concentrated into the hands of entrepreneurs, funds were available to drive innovation, thus creating new technologies and industries that added to the portfolios of the wealthy. There is much to be said for this time as foods became more widely available, technology made many tasks easier, and rural life gave way to urban living. However, the best values of agrarian society were overshadowed by increases in competitiveness, exploitation, greed, and self-indulgence.

Huge family fortunes were made as those with wealth built the factories that produced the goods that were used to establish cities, highways, rail lines, communications enterprises, and other activities of the Industrial Age. On one hand, much of this was good for society while on the other we saw the emergence of the term "robber baron." This era brought with it the significant empowerment of the corporation, a business entity that was eventually granted the same rights as those of individuals. With the power of individual rights vested unto them, and a legal mission of maximizing profits and growth for the relatively few members of society who owned them, these corporations grew, absorbed each other, and became huge multinational entities.[40]

The expansion of industrialism resulted in the formation of huge national and international banks, investment houses, stock exchanges, and an army of speculators. This movement further expanded the opportunities for corporate growth such that some corporations are now so large that their annual budgets exceed that of all but a handful of nations. Because the legal requirement of these multinational industrial and financial corporations is to achieve maximum profit and

---

[40] On January 21, 2010, the U.S. Supreme Court even granted corporations the right to spend unlimited amounts of money to ensure the election of candidates they supported, reversing 100 years of laws preventing such power over the political process.

maximum growth for their investors only, their influence on society has moved us from the agrarian principles of caring, sharing, and community to a singular focus on profits, unabashed greed, and a quest for ever-increasing growth and consumption on a planet with limited resources.

Although the attendant reductions in ethics and morality had been under the surface for many years, the events that began in September 2008 brought the problem to the front pages of newspapers around the globe. Massive financial corporations too big to fail were near collapse due to the unrestrained greed of incompetent or scheming bankers operating with a lust for profits and bonuses at the expense of the populace and the global economic system. Even after bailouts by taxpayers, this example of unrestrained carnivorous corporate capitalism remained in place as bankers continued to pass out huge bonuses while refusing to submit to audits by the government.

To add insult to injury, these special interests are so blatant that they continue to foreclose on millions of homes while taking billions in bonuses in defiance of the wishes of Congress and the people.

It is becoming more obvious that an elite class has taken reign over the common people of this country who now pay income and sales taxes, who will pay more future taxes, and who will experience higher inflation rates as more money is printed out of thin air to pay for the crimes of these bankers and to fund the schemes of Wall Street elites.[41] Many people and farmers

---

[41] On July 15, 2010 the SEC fined Goldman Sachs $550 million for their part in sub-prime mortgage scam. https://www.sec.gov/news/press/2010/2010-123.htm. On Jan. 14, 2016, it agreed to an additional $5.1 billion in settlement payments. http://fortune.com/2016/01/14/goldman-sachs-mortgage-bonds-settlement/

are now angered because they feel they are being taxed into economic servitude while their country is being stolen out from under their feet.

Today's situation is not entirely dissimilar to one other period in American history when the control of our country was in the hands of scoundrels who were feeding their own coffers with funds, fees, and taxes confiscated from the public with little return. At that time in history, it was the farmers who left their fields because they had had enough. They went forth to address the issue and remove the hands of the greedy from the throats of our countrymen and women. That was in 1775 when a farmer fired the shot heard around the world. The Revolutionary War began, and America became a country free from the grip of wealthy British royals. As we today are a country in the grip of wealthy elites, we again can remove the hand on our throat, but this time without firing a shot.

The founding principles practiced 10,000 years ago by our earliest farmers, which resulted in the emergence of civilization, and more recently in the emergence of our country, have now been supplanted by what many feel is a distorted, destructive, corporate paradigm that has brought us dangerously close to what some thinkers warn could be the end of a healthy society if not the end of civilization as we know it.

Our American farmers know this best, as they have been victims of a corporate agribusiness machine that is so huge, well-funded, and efficient that they cannot compete. Millions of family farmers have gone out of business at the hands of

---

As I make the final edits to this book o, the Securities and Exchange Commission prepares to launch a criminal investigation of Goldman Sachs, one of the world's most powerful investment firms. The charges stem from the government's allegations that Goldman Sachs sold investment products that it knew were faulty. The allegations claim that Goldman Sachs bet against these investments and made billions in profits when those investments failed.

huge agribusinesses that abandoned the agrarian principles and practices necessary to produce healthy food. These were replaced with profit-obsessed production techniques, inhumane treatment of animals to produce as much meat as possible using as little space as possible, and the advent of genetically modified crops in order to produce as much food as possible out of now depleted or dead soils.

This is evidenced by the rapid disappearance of the endangered species we know as the family farmer as well as nutrient-rich, uncontaminated, healthy food. The effects of dead, nutrient-empty food is seen in the obesity rates of our children and populace and in the declining level of health of our society as a whole.

But, as Margaret Meade notes, a small committed group of people can change the world. Farmers are the most powerful people in the world because they provide the food we eat. Despite the attempts of Monsanto and others to own the food chain through patents, farmers still have the knowledge necessary to save us from the dangers that would result if these corporations became successful. Yet despite their knowledge and power, farmers are fiercely independent and desperately disorganized. Although they compete among themselves to achieve a market advantage over their neighbor, they would extend a hand, spare nothing, and give the shirts off their backs to rebuild the same neighbor's farm after a disastrous fire or a streak of bad luck. And why? Because that same gene that enabled our ancestors to leave the security of caves for the uncertain promise of farmlands, that farmer gene that gave birth to civilization, still is firmly embedded in the character of their modern-day descendants who work so hard for the love of the earth, the farm, and their neighbors.

I believe that farmers can once again be the catalyst that can help us all take back our country and return to the civilization we need to create a sustainable economy, sustainable future, and a return to all that is good about humanity.

Because they enjoy popular respect and admiration, in stepping forward farmers can truly set an example that will encourage others to join them in a quest to open the doors to the shared economy.

Among their most ardent supporters would be millions of those who, although not as connected to the soil, embrace the core values of farmers – sharing, caring, compassion, and the quest for ultimate good.

Our opponents in the agricultural industry are very powerful and farm workers are still weak in money and influence. But we have another kind of power that comes from the justice of our cause. So long as we are willing to sacrifice for that cause, so long as we persist in non-violence and work to spread the message of our struggle, then millions of people around the world will respond from their heart, will support our efforts ... and in the end we will overcome.

~Cesar Chavez, Mexican American
farm worker/ labor leader

We do not want to find fault with each other, but to solidify our forces and say to each other: "We must be together; our masters are joined together and we must do the same thing."

~Mother Jones, American labor and
community organizer

Chapter 21 - Universities

During the past two decades, with the more recent 10 years being the most relevant, the continually deteriorating economic conditions have impacted universities in a negative way.

As administrators equate growth with success, annual budgets have skyrocketed as many new buildings appeared. Facility operations and maintenance costs surged along with faculty pay rates.

Concurrently, state funding did not increase proportionally so funding gaps became larger. As a result, administrators began to look to other areas for income. One source of income was from royalties relating to sports programs. Although lucrative, this income is unpredictable as it depends on the success of a university's various sports teams.

Another income source that benefits professors directly is that which they earn from books they write that are required reading for their students who must purchase them at costs that can exceed $100 per book. Yet this income is becoming more controversial as book costs soar and pressure grows to use the Internet to deliver information at much lower costs.

A far more enticing source of income is from royalties the university can receive by licensing technologies developed on campus to corporations to commercialize. This can bring many millions of dollars into the coffers of public research institutions. My local university, although it does pay a portion of their salaries, requires researchers to fund a very high percentage of their own research. Thus, research faculty must spend a considerable amount of time seeking government grants, corporate sponsors, or income from licensing deals, which the university shares with them. This policy of self-funding introduces into the academic agenda a financial factor that is very questionable. Because researchers must raise money to continue their work, the purity of the educational or research agenda is potentially compromised because of differences in the agendas of profit-making entities and educators.

By corporatizing the university in this manner, we open the institution to some serious potential risks and ethical dilemmas. The old paradigm of "publish or perish" has changed to "patent or perish" for research faculty. This places pressure on the university to hire new faculty members based as much on their ability to attract grants and sponsors as on their potential to educate students in the classroom. It can be a difficult balancing act for these researchers to maintain their enthusiasm for time spent with students when royalty-sharing compensation plans can earn them several hundred thousand dollars a year for technologies they are working to develop. Although some institutions might take pride in having a Nobel Laureate on their staff, the impact of these superstars on students may not be what it could. It is no secret that more and more courses at some research institutions are taught by graduate students while the more highly noted and compensated researchers focus their efforts in the laboratory developing marketable technologies.

As new technologies are developed in the laboratories of research universities, they are not all licensed immediately, thus a backlog of available technologies develops. I remember walking into the office of my friend who was directing the Commercial Ventures and Intellectual Property (CVIP) department of a university. He was sitting at his desk facing towards me behind three tall stacks of documents. The outer two were stacked higher than his head while the center pile was stacked just high enough for me to see his head. It was a rather funny sight to see only his head visible at the top of the center pile! When I asked him what this was all about, he told me they were documents detailing all the intellectual property the university had available for licensing!

I was shocked at the sheer volume of documents and it made me realize that as the amount of university owned, income producing, intellectual properties increases, the pressure to get them sold also increases. Thus, the university must bring people such as venture capitalists and corporate clients into the mix. As these people become more important funding sources, their relationships and economic power, if left unchecked, could inappropriately impact the curriculum or credibility of the university as a public educational or land-grant institution.

This was made very clear to me when I attended a meeting of university administrators, researchers, venture capitalists, and interested parties being held to discuss technology transfers. One administrator asked how the university could make itself more attractive to venture capitalists. One of the more illustrious venture capitalists who occupied center stage said, and I closely paraphrase, "Public universities, because of their institutional obligations to the community, are sometimes difficult for venture capitalists to deal with. In order to be more attractive to venture capitalists and corporate sponsors, the university must sacrifice some of its principles." I was aghast, but not surprised.

After a moment or two I, being as undiplomatic and candid as I can sometimes be, spoke up. "This is a public land grant institution that was established to serve the community. I'd have a real problem if a publicly funded institution were to develop a technology, such as a pill that my aging mother takes to prevent a re-occurrence of breast cancer, and then licenses it to a corporation who makes them for 72 cents a pill and sells them to my mother for $10 a pill! I do not believe public institutions need to bow to venture capitalists and sacrifice their principles as this man suggests. He should accept that venture capitalists need to relax their greed and need for maximum profits and growth when dealing with community owned or funded institutions." The room went stiff and silent. After what seemed for many, except me, to be an eternal moment, a friend of mine spoke up to break the silence by saying, "I've known Michael for years and you can count on him to say what he is thinking." Now don't get me wrong, I don't despise venture capitalists. In fact I was a co-founder of the Western Mass. Venture Forum, a well-respected group formed to introduce technologists to funders. I just despise greed.

Following my comments, the meeting went on in a decidedly more subdued manner, and a man I greatly respect as the Dean of the Engineering Department responded to my comment by saying, "I want to know that if a great new technology is developed in my department, there is a good chance that it will become commercialized. This requires venture capitalists." I would agree with him, but from a different point of view. I want to know that if a researcher develops a one pill cure for cancer, a new source of energy, or any disruptive technology, it will become commercialized rather than suppressed by the university or those on whom it relies for funding. As universities become more beholden to these types of funders, there is an increased danger that the direction of research or education will be impacted in a way determined more by the benefit to the bottom line of potential funders than to the benefit of the community.

Just as important, there must be a real financial return to the community itself for the tax money state or federal governments invest in universities, who then make licensing deals with those in the commercial sector. When bankers make loans, or investors fund start-up companies, the bankers get interest and the investors get a percentage of the equity in the companies. This is only fair. So it is only fair that when the community, invests tax dollars in universities that produce income from technology licenses, the community should get a return. The same is true when a government agency such as the National Science Foundation or National Institute of Health makes an investment in technology or drug companies the community should get a return.

But this is not the case. The sad fact is that the community always gets taken advantage of in these situations. For example, drug companies always tell us that drugs are so expensive because the cost of producing a new drug averages $500 million and a healthy return is required. What that drug company doesn't tell you is that often times, half, if not all of the money necessary to develop that drug came as a grant, not a loan, a grant from the National Institute for Health, a taxpayer-funded government agency! In other words, corporations use our money to create new drugs, and then sell them back to us at extraordinary prices when we were the ones who made the drug possible! This is straight out corporate welfare of the worst kind. I feel our publicly funded universities must be vigilant to maintain their integrity and to provide a real return on the public investment taxpayers make into the university. This personal opinion was reinforced at the end of the aforementioned venture capitalist meeting when a university administrator quietly walked by me in the shadows and said "What you said was very important."

Some university administrators have suggested to me that the return of the community's investment into the university was that the university was educating their children; however, I feel this is far from an acceptable answer. My own alma mater has an annual budget exceeding $200,000,000, much of which is paid for by taxpayers or students. For that it enrolls about 4,000 freshman students a year. Of that amount, a growing percentage comes from out of state. A significant portion of new entering students do not complete their educations – up to 50% by some estimates. Of those that do, many do not find work in their chosen careers, and more recently, any jobs at all; and of those that do, a good number leave the state. So it is hard to determine exactly how many of those 4,000 students actually benefit from the money we invested in the university, or how many provide services to the local community upon graduation. More recently, the cost to the student of an education has risen dramatically while the value is dropping due to economic conditions. To top all that off, many students leave school with from $25,000 to $100,000 of personal student loan debt which cannot be discharged by bankruptcy in the event of a personal economic downturn or medical tragedy![42]

Yet as this trend continues, professors making from $70,000 to $100,000 and more a year seek higher salaries and cost-of-living increases even though most of a university's budget is already being used to pay faculty salaries. Something certainly needs to be done to provide students with a better outcome, professors with a fair salary, and the community with a return on what some are beginning to describe as a questionable investment. I sense that there may be an educational bubble that could burst in the coming times.

---

[42] My recommendation is to offset the financial damage experienced by students who do not or cannot complete a college education by providing them with Certificates of Attendance that recognize the time spent and grade point average received during their time at the institution.

It is a commonly accepted belief that a college education is valuable. If these rising education costs are not supported with quantifiable evidence of their value, and in light of rising, unprecedented levels of student debt, rapidly increasing student loan default rates, and increasing difficulty in getting a good paying job, the perceived value of an advanced education could drop and the $400 billion a year education industry could suffer greatly.

In my original writings in 2000, I considered how the university would fit in as an institution in an E2M regional shared economy. I suggested that the research university was the entity that could spawn innovations that would play a large part in determining the direction of the future economy and society. I suggested, too, that teams of students I referred to as "think teams" could be established to work with E2M-certified or affiliated businesses located outside of the university walls. These think teams would interact in real time with these businesses to give them access to help, advice, research time, information gathering, and university facilities and equipment. By helping E2M community-owned businesses to become successful, the university, as an institution, would be helping to create more community wealth as a return on the investment made by community members through the taxes they pay to fund public universities. After all, the university was given life by the community, was funded by the community, and should provide real benefits to the community where possible. The university could further license E2M-certified or affiliated companies to commercialize technologies its faculty developed under grants provided by the university or other public entities such as the National Science Foundation, National Institute of Health, the US Government, and other publicly funded organizations.

The E2M strategy is such that it enables the university, as a community asset, to help these companies that are going to be giving money back to the community through the community's ownership of equity. Under this scenario, the university could be a breeding ground for E2M community-owned companies that continually grow wealth for the community.

In July of 2001, I was having lunch with a friend who had just ended his tenure as chancellor of a large university. When I related my ideas about E2M and the university's prospective role, he smiled and related a story. "For five years," he told me, "there have been many conversations on campuses across the nation and in Washington, D.C., relating to the question asking "How does the university, as an institution, engage the community?" "There has been so much talk and so little resolution," he continued, "that a joke now describes the entire dialog as 'words dancing over the landscape.' Your ideas, Michael, are among the more exciting I've heard in a long time!" I was elated and further excited when he referred me on to his friend who was the president of Hampshire College. At a later meeting with his friend, I was met with excitement, and was invited to have the first-ever private forum at the home of this man. That forum produced even more energy for E2M and was followed by a public forum at Hampshire College's Red Barn, at which time an audience responded enthusiastically to the early, not yet finalized, version of E2M. Input from that meeting along with that of the E2M.org board and local students helped me craft the final version of the model.

Further implementation of university programs to help establish a shared economy could arise as these ideas take root within some quarters at the universities. This could occur even as the corporatization of cash-strapped, publicly funded universities raises some real concerns, challenges, and threats to the integrity of the institution and its educational programs at universities.

These concerns result from increased activity between the university, corporate funders, and the Wall Street bankers who caused our current problems according to President Obama, and who still don't or won't get it.[43] These are not team players and should not be placed in any position of control or significant influence within the "hallowed halls" of our public universities.

Serious challenges exist for administrators, faculty, students, and communities as corporate dollars find their way into the coffers of universities and wallets of educators and researchers. This can influence the direction of research, education, and the nature of the relationship between the university and the community.

In a shared economy, the university as an institution maintains its primary obligation to the community by spawning companies that create wealth for entrepreneurs, employees, investors, and for the community. These companies will truly enrich the community, university, students, and faculty. In the shared economy, such companies provide as much of the community's needs as possible while relying on old economy companies as little as possible.

Thus, by working with companies dedicated to communities, research can be directed at what is best for the community rather than the bottom line of traditional companies which operate with a singular focus on profits. Public education should always be aimed at maximizing individual growth and

---

[43] Fortunately, the president recently removed private banks from their role as student loan administrators saving students $60 billion dollars in bank fees, costs, and excess interest.

independence rather than simply providing an ongoing stream of workers to perpetuate the current maximum profit and growth paradigm that is so problematic. A shared economy will help to ensure that end is met.

Today, the solitary inventor, tinkering in his shop, has been overshadowed by task forces of scientists in laboratories and testing fields. The prospect of domination of the nation's scholars by Federal employment, project allocations, and the power of money is ever present – and is gravely to be regarded.

~President Dwight D. Eisenhower
Farewell Address; January 17, 1961

I know of no safe repository of the ultimate power of society but people. And if we think them not enlightened enough, the remedy is not to take the power from them, but to inform them by education.

~Thomas Jefferson

Chapter 22 - Governments

When I first made the commitment to establish the E2M economic model, I decided that I should identify those who I felt could be opposed to the idea of an alternative economic system, and I decided to call on them. The first group I spoke with were elected officials, thinking that an empowered and wealthy community might be perceived as a threat to the government. I was pleasantly surprised when I had conversations with Massachusetts State Representative Benjamin Swan and Congressman John V. Olver. Each of them applauded the E2M idea and asked that representatives from their offices be placed on my board of directors. Ben joined the E2M board along with Jon Niedzielski, District Director for Congressman Olver, followed shortly thereafter by Mary Jane Bacon, a senior aide from the office of then Massachusetts State Senate President pro tempe Stan Rosenberg. This brought the size of the board to six, including Steve Rogers, Courtney Raiph, and me. At that point, I felt we had enough government representation.

What I have learned is that the government has the potential to become a great partner with E2M. Those elected officials with whom I worked want E2M to succeed. Most newly elected officials have the same hopes for their constituents as do those people now involved with E2M. Once elected to office, some manage to remain hopeful and true to their beliefs while others become co-opted by the influence of well-heeled contributors, lobbyists, or other human weaknesses. In a shared economy, those elected officials who have a greater vision for their constituents would be able to develop a great partnership with the wealthy communities they represent and who elected them, thus, could become less beholden to wealthy private interests.

Government could be a most powerful force in advancing the shared economy by providing tax benefits to those individuals who invest in E2M certified or affiliated companies. This could include tax-free status for E2M-related investment income, tax credits, and other strategies to empower E2M investors and companies. As Mary Jane Bacon of the E2M board once described it, E2M companies are a hybrid between for-profit companies and nonprofits. Although profitability is very important, an E2M company has a community benefit similar to nonprofits and such companies and the investors who fund them could receive special treatment as do nonprofits and those who donate to them.

The E2M Regional Economic Councils could also act as a quasi-governmental body that could implement certain strategies and programs that do not fit well within the government or corporate sector. Examples would include programs that are so vital to a sustainable community and healthy populace that they cannot be relegated to those who would use them to maximize profits and growth for the few. Such programs could include a public health insurance program, scientific research and development programs aimed at maximizing benefits to the community, low-interest or non-interest-bearing mortgage programs, and other initiatives.

The term corporate welfare comes to mind here, too. Many corporations receive grants from the National Institute for Health, the National Science Foundation, the military, and other agencies. The government often receives no benefit from their investments because the government is deemed to be a body that should not own corporations. This may be appropriate on some levels, but in many other instances the government could channel corporate welfare funds through E2M Regional Councils, which could then move the funds into corporate coffers as loans or in return for equity. This would result in funds getting to corporations who might need them, but would be fairer to the community in that it would receive equity for these corporate grants just as a private investor would when making venture investments into corporations. In this manner, the taxpayer funds collected by the government could help expand the E2M system of community-owned companies while the government maintains an arm's-length distance from private enterprise. This could do much to redirect the income now lost to corporate welfare programs back to the community.

The best thing the government could do if it wanted to assist opening the doors to the shared economy is to pass local, state, or federal legislation that recognizes the E2M infrastructure as a valid organization representing the financial interests of the community. With that increased credibility, the relationship between the E2M Regional Economic Councils and other publicly funded entities such as universities, nonprofits, human service agencies, and other institutions could be further legitimized and strengthened to develop important community benefit programs.

As I've said before, the establishment of E2M and the shared economy does not require the approval of the government or the passage of any legislation. However, as a body that is aligned with the best interests of the public, the government can be a powerful force to accelerate the rate at which the shared economy becomes established.

Hope is the bedrock of this nation; the belief that our destiny will not be written for us, but by us; by all those men and women who are not content to settle for the world as it is; who have courage to remake the world as it should be.

~Barack Obama, January 3, 2008

The strongest bond of human sympathy outside the family relation should be one uniting working people of all nations and tongues and kindred.

~Abraham Lincoln

Each time a person stands up for an ideal, or acts to improve the lot of others, or strikes out against injustice, he sends forth a tiny ripple of hope, and crossing each other from a million different centers of energy and daring, these ripples build a current that can sweep down the mightiest walls of oppression and resistance.

~Robert F. Kennedy

Chapter 23 - Emerging Nations

I believe the U.S. could be the hardest place to create a new economic movement, but I am hopeful. In writing this book, it is also hoped that it will land on the right desk of the right person in another country looking for a rational, capital-based, free-market economic system.

Following the fall of the Berlin Wall, the leaders of formerly Communist countries were seeking information on how to structure a free-market economy in their countries. Russian leaders, in particular, invited American economists to offer suggestions and to teach the basics of American capitalism.

Of course, as a former Communist state, how could we expect them to understand that they were inviting exactly the wrong people? The Russians explored corporate structures such as employee stock ownership plans (ESOPs) and the like. However the end result over the decades has been that many in the Russian populace have become disenchanted with their economic system, a thriving black market has developed, and great power fell into the hands of a small but powerful economic class. As this became a threat to social and governmental stability, friction grew, jailing commenced, and the possibility of a return to the old ways has become more commonly discussed.

The E2M model can offer what Russia and emerging countries seek, a realistic free-market economic system of community capitalism that does not lead to a situation in which one percent of the population owns most of the private property.

In these past months, it is obvious that Russia is not the only country in need of a viable economic system. Recent sociopolitical activities in Iceland, Cuba, Egypt, Libya, Tunisia, Syria, Greece, Italy and other countries indicate a new era of freedom is arising. By considering E2M as an economic model, these countries can establish long-term sustainability, a balance of economic control between the government and the people, and a significant economic and social advantage over countries that have fallen victim to those who misuse capitalism.

Other countries that particularly come to mind are the former Soviet states and a number of countries in Central and South America and the South Pacific. I make particular reference to the seven governments of the ALBA economic and social alliance in Latin America which, on April 17, 2009, signed the Document of the Bolivarian Alternative for the Peoples of Our Americas (ALBA) in response to the proposed Declaration of the 5th Summit of the Americas.[44] These countries include Bolivia, Cuba, Dominica, Ecuador, Honduras, Nicaragua, and Venezuela.

I believe that the abandonment of the model based on maximizing profit and growth for the few, in favor of the E2M economic system, would give rise to competitive national economies that would enable emerging countries to become formidable, sustainable players on the global stage.

The acceptance of the new paradigm would also produce a quality of life that would help to instill an appreciation for a simpler, less exploitative, more leisurely lifestyle. I believe this model could help create societal happiness without the need to spend enormous amounts of money and resources to

---

[44] http://www.globalresearch.ca/index.php?context=va&aid=13243

create needs and markets for products that promise happiness but produce more debt, waste, and pollution than happiness.

I now understand that my welfare is only possible if I acknowledge my unity with all the people of the world without exception.

~Leo Tolstoy, Russian author of *War and Peace*

Now my friends, I am opposed to the system of society in which we live today, not because I lack the natural equipment to do for myself but because I am not satisfied to make myself comfortable knowing that there are thousands of my fellow men who suffer for the barest necessities of life. We were taught under the old ethic that man's business on this earth was to look out for himself. That was the ethic of the jungle; the ethic of the wild beast. Take care of yourself, no matter what may become of your fellow man. Thousands of years ago the question was asked: "Am I my brother's keeper?" That question has never yet been answered in a way that is satisfactory to civilized society. Yes, I am my brother's keeper. I am under a moral obligation to him that is inspired, not by any maudlin sentimentality but by the higher duty I owe myself. What would you think me if I were capable of seating myself at a table and gorging myself with food and saw about me the children of my fellow beings starving to death?

~Eugene V. Debs, Indiana State Senator, in a 1908 speech

Chapter 24 - The Wealthy

As I've said in lectures over the years, the wealthy are victims of an unsustainable economic system, too; it just takes longer for them to find out. On one level, their wealth comes from the community. If the community is not healthy, the commercial sector cannot remain healthy, and the wealthy will take losses.[45] On another level, if our economy unravels in as dramatic a fashion as is possible and inevitable, the level of social unrest could rise. This has occurred a number of times in the past; and just because we have been experiencing a century of calm in the U.S., does not mean things can't change rapidly.

The words in the second paragraph of the Declaration of Independence apply not only to governments as a controlling force over citizens; it applies to any system. The financial system is no exception. I am afraid that the wealthy, as the primary beneficiaries of the financial system, are exposed to much more potential disruption than they may believe. The populace is being pushed to the limits of their comfort zone. The wealthy have great potential to help release the pressure or to look the other way and try to maintain the status quo until the matter is out of their hands.

Although the enormous concentration of wealth in such few hands is a principal cause of today's problems, I must say it is not necessarily the fault of the wealthy. Most of them do not

---

[45] This was shown to be accurate when the consumer sector shut down starting in September 2008, triggering an economic crisis. What I did not expect was the bailouts of the wealthy that occurred following that collapse. However, the wealthy are only temporary beneficiaries of a bailout because public anger has increased dramatically and any future bailouts will only trigger more resentment. This could result in dramatic political repercussions for elected officials as well as social unrest.

proactively create the damage the current economic system does to millions of people. It is the manner in which their wealth is used that is the problem. A large percentage of the wealthy do not look after their own investments. They are too busy having fun, living lives of comfort, and partaking in the advantages of wealth to bother themselves with the ominous task of maximizing their incomes. That is left to investment bankers, stock brokerages, and other financial institutions run by less wealthy, but far more self-serving and ruthless individuals than the wealthy themselves.

These financial advisors make their own money from commissions, transaction fees, profit-sharing or other fees received from facilitating venture investments, stock trades, loans, etc. These are the individuals who not only run credit card companies that charge 33% interest rates on funds they borrow from the Federal Reserve for 1% or less. They also run brokerage houses and banks that accept billions in bailouts, then pay billions in bonuses, saddle their customers with $38 billion of overdraft charges a year, and do the other things to "serve" their wealthy clients[46] and investors.

In 2000, most of this investment activity was transacted through six large brokerage houses and international banks. A friend of mine who once managed $100,000,000 at one of those companies tells of $150 lunches where fund managers made sweetheart deals among each other on investment strategies. Thus, the manner in which the funds of the wealthy impact society are determined by relatively few people while their wealthy clients attend to other matters like enjoying life to its fullest free from financial worries.

---

[46] These are the same people and organizations that received enormous bailouts and bonuses in the recent economic collapse.

People who have developed new or unanticipated wealth often find themselves drawn into this infrastructure of financial advisors regardless of their personal ethical or moral beliefs. One person I know went from a moderate income with few assets to an extraordinary income with assets exceeding hundreds of millions of dollars. I asked this person what the most significant personal change was as a result of this rather sudden wealth. This person said, "The pressure to make sure that my investments produce every penny they possibly can."

This message is constantly kept in the minds of the wealthy by those whose job it is to administer wealth. Of course, maximizing trading volume and the wealth of the rich is also in the best interests of the financial advisors who make money on trading commissions. However, it is becoming more obvious that this idea that you must make as much for your client as possible is a bankrupt policy. It ultimately leads to social and financial inequities, unsustainability, conflict, or worse.

This is not only true for advocates for the wealthy, but for anyone advocating for a particular group. This can include those who negotiate for maximum compensation plans for CEOs and other managers, or for workers under collective bargaining, or even between two people under the advice of lawyers. All of these advocates, as well as their clients, must understand when enough is enough, especially when more than enough can lead to unsustainability or worse. I personally do not share the contempt some people have for the wealthy. I'd like to see all of us become financially independent or rich. There is definitely a place in the shared economy for those who are wealthy. They have much to offer and much to benefit.

It is time for those of wealth to take more responsibility over their investments; indifference is no longer an option. They need not be excessively reliant on their financial advisors and could use their own power more wisely. Investing in local E2M and shared economy initiatives, seeking out socially responsible investment advisors, or increasing their charitable activities would be a good place to start.

I believe we will find a good number of wealthy people who will come on board with us. These may not be the older entrenched wealthy; they could easily come from among the middle-age or young generation who inherited their wealth. I know a number of these folks and find there is a level of guilt some of them feel for having wealth in the face of so much suffering in the world. Some question the manner in which their wealth was created, considering some of it is many generations old and may have been created at the expense of Native Americans, or built on slavery or the suffering of poorly treated employees, or whose creation caused environmental damage that would not be tolerated in today's world. Although I can understand their guilt, I think it serves no purpose, especially when they could easily use their money for the betterment of society while maintaining the financial security and independence their wealth brings them. These are the younger people of wealth who are more likely to impart some of their wealth to the health and well-being of their community. They are less likely to hold so tightly to their wealth based on old ideas and organizations destined for failure. They are of the new age.

The good we secure for ourselves is precarious and uncertain until it is secured for all of us and incorporated into our common life.

~Jane Addams, American Nobel Laureate

A true revolution of values will soon cause us to question the fairness and justice of many of our past and present policies. On the one hand, we are called to play the Good Samaritan on life's roadside, but that will be only an initial act. One day we must come to see that the whole Jericho Road must be transformed so that men and women will not be constantly beaten and robbed as they make their journey on life's highway. True compassion is more than flinging a coin to a beggar. It comes to see that an edifice which produces beggars needs restructuring.

~Martin Luther King, Jr.

Chapter 25 - Where Do We Go From Here?

A number of the predictions I made in 1999 and 2000 have now come to pass. Economic uncertainty has increased since September 2008 when global financial institutions teetered on the edge of collapse. That collapse was not a surprise to those who read my earlier writings, which predicted that consumers would eventually stop buying products when they reached their limit of indebtedness. I warned that loss of consumer activity could result in the demise of the system and the flight of domestic investments to foreign venues. Although this did happen in September 2008, much to my surprise the government stepped in and actually spent trillions of our future tax dollars to bail out and appease the very same bankers who caused the problems in the first place!

The unfortunate fact is that the underlying problems have not been eliminated and there will be more economic crises to come during the next decade or sooner. We must prepare now to protect ourselves and our personal values, as well as our freedoms and our liberties. There has never been a better time to create a new economic system of, by and for the people. We cannot change the old system. We must not try to overthrow it; it is already dying. We cannot depend on the government to take care of the situation, or to take care of us. We must realize the government will not keep us safe, it will always act in the best interests of those who control the capital. Unsettling events are likely to unfold as they already have in other countries such as France, Greece, Ireland, Malaysia, Thailand, and other areas that are under great social and economic stress.

As things unfold, we will eventually realize that we, as individuals, are on our own. Therefore we must depend on ourselves by doing those things we can achieve on our own. We can avoid significant amounts of negative energy, restrictive governmental reactions, and even social unrest or violence by taking the nonviolent and easier path this book suggests. We can take easily implementable actions whose success we, as a people, can guarantee, and which will give us the world we want without any battles fought, any blood shed, or any time lost in a world in which time is limited and urgency is required.

As the true nature of the current economic system and the motives of those who control it become known, it becomes more obvious that we are at a fork in the path of the human journey and our future depends on which path we choose. We will either be a populace subject to the actions of a big government controlled by big business in this Corporate Age, or we will become a powerful populace moving ahead to a bright future of self-determination and a smaller, truly democratic government controlled by communities as we enter the age of the shared economy.

Using the E2M model, a small percentage of the populace can create great change with minimal inputs. If only five percent of people joined the E2M initiative we could create a "critical mass" of economic power significant enough to launch a new economic paradigm that could begin the transformation process and help launch the shared economy.

The introduction of a shared economy would result in a new era that would be more idyllic and leisurely. The speed of society and pace of daily activities would slow down. While the most important things would still be getting done, those things that should be important, yet which have been diminished by the current system, would become important again. Such things are time with our families, friends, and neighbors. Volunteering, vacationing, and maybe even voting! Spiritual renewal, saving money for the future, a simpler way of living, and a reemergence of widespread sanity! All in all, a dignified, debt-free, less burdensome lifestyle for everyone.

The economic and environmental news of the day underscores the fact that there is very little precious time left to waste. The time for change is upon us; the door to the shared economy is within our reach. It is time to assemble ourselves as community members to create the great and wonderful changes possible.

In this endeavor, we all have something to gain and we are equally important and deserving. We cannot allow ourselves to be separated by labels or characteristics such as left or right, man or woman, black or white, conservative or liberal, straight, gay, bisexual, trans, Republican, Democrat, Christian, Muslim, Jewish, Buddhist, educated or uneducated. The sad fact is that 99% of us are bound together by one common thread – we are all victims of the current economic system.

The shared economy is not about any of those things that separate us as a united people, it is about connecting with each other as we seek what is right for all of us. It is about ethics, honor, love, recapturing the spirit of our humanity, and unchaining ourselves from those who seek to control us for their own selfish reasons.

The E2M model is not about politics or religion or any of those types of things. It is about economics only; it is about the money and the economic power it brings. It is about achieving the economic power necessary to take hold of the future we all deserve. Our mission is not to advocate for any of the other things that separate us, lest we defeat ourselves before we save ourselves. Those things that separate us are the mortar that holds together the walls built by others to contain us as mere laborers, debtors, mortgagees, or subservient subjects.

It will be easier to discuss and resolve those things that separate us when the ills caused by our current economic system are cured and when we are feeling better and more hopeful. Even then, on some issues, we will never agree, but the world will be a friendlier place for those who agree to disagree.

For now, we must unite around the fact that each and every one of us does not want children to go to bed hungry, to feel hopeless growing up, to watch anyone lose their home to a heartless system, or to lose the opportunity to eat healthy food because family farmers are going out of business.

If we truly want a shared economy, it is because we want a better, more hopeful world for each other, not just for ourselves. To achieve that, we must rely on that basic human goodness that is predominant in any people.

We must gather together and create the wind under our wings that we need so we can fly, so we can join together as one, connected by our hearts and hopes for something greater.

We must speak as a united force with great economic power in order to create that society that is within our reach. And we must do it now.

The next stage of humanity is at hand and it is up to us as common people to decide what it looks like. If it a continuation of the greed-driven, consumption-based system that benefits the few at the expense of the many and the planet, then we will see a tragic future.

Alternatively, we can sustain a shared economy based on connecting, caring, sharing, simpler living, and love to take us far into this millennium and even beyond.

It is our best chance to create the destiny God has made available to us.

We are at the door to the shared economy.
We can no longer remain silent.
The time is ripe.
It is ours for the taking!

I cannot believe that the inscrutable universe turns on an axis of suffering; surely the strange beauty of the world must somewhere rest on pure joy!
~Louise Bogan, U.S. Poet Laureate

Sanity may be madness but the maddest of all is to see life as it is and not as it should be. ~From *Don Quixote*

I've been put on the planet to serve humanity. I have to remind myself to live simply and not to overindulge, which is a constant battle in a material world.
~Sandra Cisneros, writer

People, even more than things, have to be restored, renewed, revived, reclaimed, and redeemed; never throw out anyone. ~Audrey Hepburn

Chapter 26 - Reviewing Our Progress Since 2000

It was at 11AM on January 1, 2000, the first day of the new millennium that I first articulated a blueprint for the E2M economic model and registered the domain name E2M.org. Since that time, many have come to believe that the E2M model can enable us to open the doors to the shared economy and a much more equitable and sustainable human era. During the next three months I produced the first written material describing my vision. I distributed only 25 copies of that booklet and found support for these ideas. As more people gathered and others joined in, we began to create E2M.org, the nonprofit organization necessary to forward the E2M mission. During the next year we established the core board of directors of E2M.org as detailed in the opening paragraphs of this book.

During the next three years, I spoke about E2M and sustainable economics at numerous venues. These included several at the UMass-Amherst; the nearby Hampshire College in the home of the college president as well as at the Red Barn public venue; the UMass-Amherst Student Government Association; the Boston Social Forum; the UMass Center for Popular Economics International Summer Institute; the National City Planners Conference in Holyoke, Mass.; the Powershift Conference in Boston; and in numerous classroom discussions.

Having established credible support, a group of us formed the E2M Organizing Committee to establish E2M as a very real system rather than an academic exercise. This required us to make connections with students, to establish the first E2M Regional Economic Council representing the community, and to create by-laws, articles of organization, policies, procedures, and methods to give life, legitimacy, and structure to the new E2M regional shared economy in Western Massachusetts. We crafted documents, websites, brochures, and video presentations, then secured Federal 501(c)(3) nonprofit status. This took more than seven years of volunteer time at weekly meetings attended most notably by Mary Westervelt, David Bisson, and his father, Ed Bisson.

In February 2008, the E2M.org board decided that it would be important to establish an industrial base to help support the E2M system as we continued our work on the E2M.org infrastructure. Having the most commercial experience, I moved ahead in several directions during the next two months. That effort culminated in March 2008 with the board crafting a vision statement based on my recommendations. These recommendations were based on the realization that the most important elements of a new sustainable society would be a sustainable agricultural sector and a renewable non-fossil energy sector operating within the E2M sustainable economy for the common good.

My final recommendation called for the use of renewable fuels to generate electricity to power indoor inner-city farms in which we could grow organic, nutrient-dense crops under lights in a highly controlled environment. This enterprise would be in inner-city buildings employing inner-city youth and residents at living wages of $16 to $20 an hour with benefits and profit-sharing. This could be the new manufacturing sector in America, in which healthy food could be available locally year-round in cities and surrounding environs, completely free from the threats of weather, environmental change, pathogens, acid rain, mercury, diesel soot, GMO pollen, or other negative elements.

The board accepted my suggestions and crafted a vision statement embracing these ideas. Due to my industrial and manufacturing history, the task of commercializing these concepts fell on to me. The board decided to reduce its activity level until I could report back showing progress in effecting the vision.

I had my marching orders. During the next six years I identified all the technological assets or companies that could serve as a consortium to form this agricultural and renewable energy industrial base.

During that time, with the help of my wife, Irene, we established a small proof-of-concept indoor growing facility to produce herbs for a local food coop. I formed a small entity we called Cityfarms Produce, which become the first indoor growing facility to be granted a USDA Organic certification in the Commonwealth of Massachusetts. Irene operated that facility for two years to prove its viability before I became more focused on the renewable fuels component of the vision.

After eliminating wind and solar power as feasible inner-city energy sources, I discovered a new technology developed by a biofuel company in Mississippi. Using this technology, formally known as catalytic vacuum pyrolysis (CVP), one is able to introduce any form of biomass and any one of several proprietary catalysts into an evacuated heated reaction chamber to initiate a process known as depolymerization. The biomass used as feedstock for the CVP process can be a number of substances ranging from clean wood chips and non-food energy crops to agricultural, municipal, organic, and sewage waste streams.

As the feedstock is acted upon within the reaction chamber, the carbon, hydrogen, oxygen, and nitrogen components separate then reform into hydrocarbon chains of light to heavy biogases, then light to heavy bio-oils. What remains is a mass of biochar containing a very high amount of carbon that formerly existed in the atmosphere as the carbon in carbon dioxide.

The bio-oils may be sold as alternative fuels to reduce the use of fossil-based fuels, the biogases may be used to power the generators to run the facility, and the biochar may be used as activated charcoal and a soil additive that can be used with other minerals and microbes to help replenish depleted lands and make them productive and fertile. Further, because the biochar is composed of the same carbon the biomass absorbed from the atmosphere as CO_2, that carbon actually removes that global warming gas for millennia and sequesters it in the soil! Thus the process helps remove global warming gases from the atmosphere and reduces the rate of climate change!

Unfortunately, the inventor was not a great businessman, which is often true of inventors, and he got himself into financial and legal problems relating to the company he had formed to commercialize his process. Having become very good friends with him, and having been taught and granted full use of the process, I even took the position of chairman of the board of another public company that was exclusively licensed to use the process.

Six months after I took control of the company, I arranged for a joint venture whereby the University of California at Santa Cruz would be provided with a fully operating facility which, in cooperation with the local community and other partners, would produce biofuels from municipal solid waste. I knew this would lead to the success of the company, but the owner of the controlling stock was an anti-academic and refused to cooperate, so I resigned the position after six months.

One year later, the inventor died in his sleep, his companies failed, and the factory and machinery was seized by the courts and granted to creditors. A group of his former employees raised a small sum to purchase the assets from the creditors and I was asked to lead an effort to save the technology for the world. I agreed, helped form a new company, and then raised another million dollars from Asian investors, since there was little support for such technologies in America or Massachusetts at the time. I rebuilt the company in Holyoke, Mass. Eighteen months later, shortly after demonstrating its capabilities to a delegation from Indonesia and China, the Asian investors and one English partner, who had controlling interests in the company, voted to move the facility to Asia. Thus, the facility was lost to America; however I am rebuilding the facility with no partners and it will serve as the energy component of the E2M industrial base.

Once this industrial base is complete, we plan to produce bio-oils, bio-gas, and biochar from renewable wood pellets and wood chips as well as from virgin, agricultural, non-food crops. These green fuels will provide the electricity to power our envisioned indoor farms to produce organic, nutrient-dense foods locally in cities throughout the country.

Biochar will be available to enrich our indoor soils as well as to enable outdoor farmers to increase their yields and the quality of crops they grow. The activated biochar will also be used to remove phosphorous and nitrogen contaminants from agricultural animal waste streams; to clean lake, river and other water of algae contaminants; to reclaim lands lost to mining activities; and for many other uses. The environmental impact will be positive on many levels. Most importantly, the process, as a whole, will be carbon-negative because it removes global warming gases from the environment.

Although we have laid a solid foundation in Western Massachusetts, it is important to reach out beyond our own region to other areas where these ideas will resonate strongly. Thus we are in discussions with entrepreneurs and investors in and outside of the USA to expand this technological base, which will be linked to the shared economy system.

As these efforts move forward, we will reconstruct our website to bring it current and more viable. The revised website will include provisions for community members to register as E2M supporters who will purchase products from future E2M-certified companies wishing to join the shared economy. As we gather more and more names of community members, the incentive for companies to join this movement will increase and the journey will increase in speed.

For those interested in our progress, please send an email to
< info@e2m.org >

It's important to know that words don't move mountains. Work, exacting work moves mountains.

~Danilo Dolci, Sicilian social activist and poet

The greatest danger for most of us is not that our aim is too high and we miss it, but that it is too low and we reach it.

~Michelangelo

Chapter 27 - Forming Your Own Regional Economic Council

I hope this book will inspire others to consider establishing Regional Economic Councils in their local regions. Due to the political and economic forces at play, it is possible the systems will soon be set in place to prevent the solutions in this book from being implemented by the people.

Time is of the essence if we hope to implement the many possibilities available within a shared economy. It is important to gather more supporters who are necessary to establish such a shared economy. If you are one of the visionaries we are hoping for, then it is very easy for you to take the first step.

If you contact us at info@e2m.org, we will send you all of the by-laws, articles of organization, policies, and procedures you need to form an E2M regional shared economy in your region, state, or country. All you need to do is look the materials over, find seven other people who have a vision for the shared economy, and we will begin to process your chartering application.

Once you are on your feet, we will advise you on how to become even more independent by applying for status as a federally chartered 501(c)(3) nonprofit organization. This will require you to select an initial board of eight directors and to produce bylaws. E2M.org will provide you with the information necessary to select your board of directors as well as with bylaws created during its past 15 years of effort. You will always be an independent organization, controlled by the residents of your region, and linked to E2M.org and other shared economy Regional Economic Councils as we expand the shared economy network based on the E2M economic model.

We will be here to help you operate in the manner necessary to succeed and maintain your E2M.org charter. We seek not to control you, but to support you. As we all succeed and our shared economy grows, we will teach each other so we can all benefit. As our commercial and industrial base expands, and our message is heard by more people, we will make efforts to include your region as we continue to spin off new shared economy E2M-certified businesses that will thrive from increasing consumer support.

As one Regional Economic Council turns to two, then ten, then many, both in the USA and other regions beyond our borders, we will surely be on our way to the future that has been prophesied by many of our spiritual and visionary leaders and can work for all of us.

Chapter 28 - The Process of Change

It must be said that change, although exciting, brings certain tensions within us as we move into a transition. As the old system dies, we will see that its end was inevitable; however there will be a sense of loss and even mourning. As we ultimately "let it go," some of us might experience anger or fear. But we will realize we must move forward for the sake of ourselves and particularly our children. That realization, along with our humanity, will see us through this phase.

As we leave the old and move towards the new, there will be a period of adjustment, re-orientation, and creativity. Although things can be a bit confusing, our innate problem-solving capacity and creativity will begin to establish the new reality.

Finally as we break through to the shared economy, we will experience a sense of renewal, relief, and great opportunity. There will be some concern that we may regress to the past, but we will prevail as the elements of the shared economy solidify and we envelop ourselves in the new reality.[47]

This process of change will most likely not be universal at first. Certain areas of the country or world and certain demographic groups may be more suited for a transition into the shared economy. In time, others will join.

---

[47] A good resource to understand the process of change is *Managing Transitions: Making the Most of Change*, William Bridges, 1991, DeCapo Press

This is typical of movements that usually begin with one or a few individuals who may be viewed as crazy. Then the first followers join in as the earliest advocates. That then brings more followers who are observing the growth of the movement. Finally will come those who are initially detached, then upon observing the growth of the movement join in so they will not be left out.

The time for great change is upon us; humanity must move in a new direction; we have everything that is necessary to accomplish this. Humankind is at an historical milestone. If we do what is necessary the world will never be the same. A great new beginning beckons and we must answer its call.

The shared economy is ours for the taking!

Change will not come if we wait for some other person or some other time. We are the ones we've been waiting for. We are the change that we seek.

~Barack Obama

Chapter 29 – Some Personal Thoughts on E2M

It has always been my goal to see E2M established to serve those who might benefit most – you. I accepted this mission to deliver this information, which came to me after I closed my last factory and opened myself up to new paths.

I was fortunate to be able to make the sacrifices necessary to pursue this end. I've met and worked with many wonderful people during the past 16 years developing the supporters, policies, information, procedures, and tools to enable you to establish an E2M Regional Economic Council in your region.

I have had the pleasure of working with many passionate people for more than a decade to forward the E2M economic model and to help others to understand it in writing this book. But it is ultimately up to you to decide if it has value to you.

In writing this book and establishing a pilot E2M Regional Economic Council in Western Massachusetts, I now feel it is up to others to decide if it resonates with them enough to see E2M implemented on a broader basis. My work and words can only set the foundation for those who care enough to embrace a shared economy and make it happen in their regions.

E2M is not about me; it cannot be about me. If it were to become about me, it would fail. It must be about you. Thus, I have no desire to be the leader of a great new movement, yet I want to see such a movement arise.

I am interested only in seeing many leaders sprout up far and wide. It is only with many leaders that the shared economy can take hold. If, in fact, those leaders appear and they use the immense power of E2M, they will realize that they have the ability to achieve things far greater than they might have imagined.

If the shared economy comes about, it will be as a result of the efforts of you and other leaders, more so than from those of my own. May we all open the doors to the shared economy.

It is ours if we want it. It is ours for the taking.

I never had much faith in leaders. I am willing to be charged with almost anything, rather than to be charged with being a leader. I am suspicious of leaders, and especially of the intellectual variety. Give me the rank and file every day in the week. If you go to the city of Washington, and you examine the pages of the Congressional Directory, you will find that almost all of those corporation lawyers and politicians or members of Congress claim, in glowing terms, that they have risen from the ranks to places of eminence and distinction. I am very glad I cannot make that claim for myself. I would be ashamed to admit that I had risen from the ranks. When I rise it will be with the ranks, and not from the ranks.
~Eugene V. Debs, Indiana State Senator,1880

I start with the premise that the function of leadership is to produce more leaders, not more followers.

~Ralph Nader, consumer activist

Chapter 30 - Parting Thoughts

There is one thing stronger
than all the armies in the world,
and that is an idea whose time has come.

~Victor Hugo

Imagine all the people,
sharing all the world...
You may say that I'm a dreamer,
but I'm not the only one...
I hope someday you'll join us,
and the world will live as one

~John Lennon

Author's Biography

In 1964, Michael Garjian left the farm for the university with a dream to become an inventor. From 1969 to 1999, he was granted nine worldwide patents and employed more than 400 people in his companies in the U.S. and Australia, manufacturing and distributing his inventions globally. In 1999, after concluding his manufacturing career at Neon Technology Corporation to become a social entrepreneur, he was offered the position of Director of Small Business Development at the nonprofit Valley Community Development Corporation in Western Massachusetts. From 2000 to 2005, he helped low-income entrepreneurs launch more than 60 small businesses. In May 2003, *Businesswest Magazine*, a major business journal, credited his office with being one of the three most significant catalysts in the economic renaissance of the city of Easthampton, Massachusetts. In 2003, he was awarded the Community Capital (formerly Western Mass. Enterprise Fund) award as "Friend of the Year" for his work.

Garjian worked with the Alliance to Develop Power, a group of 10,000 very low-income individuals occupying tenant-owned apartment complexes throughout Western Mass. He helped them form a worker-owned cooperative to provide landscape and painting services to their properties. He worked with tenant organizations to help them better understand how to use their $40,000,000 in financial power to achieve their social goals. In 2002 he was awarded the Alliance's Champion of the Year award for his work.

As a consultant to sustainable energy companies, he worked closely with the U.S. Environmental Protection Agency, Massachusetts Department of Environmental Protection, members of the Massachusetts and North Carolina state legislatures, and the city of Cincinnati, Ohio to help develop programs relating to renewable fuels.

Garjian is a principal in several companies involved in sustainable energy and agriculture, with a focus on advanced biofuels, wind power, and indoor agriculture. He currently works with family farmer-owned coops to produce carbon-smart agricultural products to restore food quality and soil vitality while removing carbon from the atmosphere.

As a volunteer at Ascentria Care Alliance, an organization that helps resettle refugees and other New Americans into their new homeland, he worked with ACA's Micro-Enterprise Service program to help some of these New Americans establish small business in order to become self-sufficient.

As a proponent of wind power, Garjian was one of three winners of the *Scientific American Magazine's* "Ten World Changing Videos" contest in 2010.

He has been a member of the board of directors of several nonprofit organizations as well as for-profit private or publicly traded corporations.

On January 1, 2000, Garjian founded E2M.org (www.e2m.org) to establish E2M, an Economic Model for Millennium 2000, a sustainable, free-market economic model based on an investment goal of adequate profits and sustainable growth for the common good.

He led the establishment of a pilot E2M regional shared economy in Western Massachusetts and has received the support of local and federal elected officials, economists, educators, students, clergy, labor leaders, entrepreneurs, and community members.

As the author of *Community Capitalism*, he offers the reader a detailed road map on how to use the E2M Economic Model to open the doors to the shared economy, in which a network of benevolent, decentralized, sustainable, regional, economic communities can become the dominant financial power that determines the destiny of our society and planet.

Made in the USA
Middletown, DE
10 April 2017